Biblical Stories:
The Truth
in
Perspective

WHAT WE SHOULD DO IN HONOR OF GOD

Anthony J. Vance

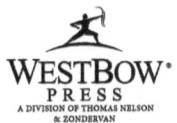

WESTBOW
PRESS
A DIVISION OF THOMAS NELSON
& ZONDERVAN

FIRST EDITION

WestBow Press books may be ordered through booksellers or by contacting:

WestBow Press
A Division of Thomas Nelson & Zondervan
1663 Liberty Drive
Bloomington, IN 47403
www.westbowpress.com
1 (866) 928-1240

Scripture taken from the King James Version of the Bible.

ISBN: 978-1-4908-4409-1 (sc)

Library of Congress Control Number: 2014912401

Printed in the United States of America.

WestBow Press rev. date: 08/19/2014

CONTENTS

AUTHOR'S NOTE

This book has been a long time in coming. Since the very first time I read the Holy Bible from cover to cover, I have been fascinated with the stories in this miraculous book called the Holy Bible. There is no subject that can be discussed, by any two people, that is not covered in the Holy Scriptures.

Many years ago after reading the entire Bible for the first time, a yearning to write about what I discovered in the Bible has been building inside of me. It has taken a long time to complete this work, written for all people, of all ethnicities, wherever they live. We are all distant cousins, and need to know the truth about our past, in order to secure our future, that is, our eternal existence.

It is with great pleasure that I present this book to you. All that is written on these pages has been studied, strictly from the Holy Scriptures. While I have consulted with learned men and women of the faith, I have not allowed their input into the writings presented before you. Their advice has been utilized to assure proper Biblical structure and alignment, to the Word of God. However, the strong viewpoint and approach this author has taken is solely his style of writing, as inspired from on High. Furthermore, I have not gathered information from theologians, whom, of which, many have studied themselves out of the faith. In writing from the great stories of the Holy Bible, my guide has been the Spirit of God. If there is anything, I know, it is that all things come secondary to God. I have prayed for the Holy Spirit to guide me in wisdom, knowledge, and in understanding, to make this collection of stories an inspiration for all who read them to increase their awareness of many untold mysteries the Holy Scriptures contain.

I would like to encourage and challenge you to follow your heart, as you read these great stories of the Holy Bible. Open your eyes and see the truth of the Scriptures. The truth shall set you free. Allow the Holy Spirit to lead you as you study the word. In searching the Scriptures, all things will be revealed unto you. As you read this book, have your Bible available also. Use the two in conjunction with one another.

These Bible lessons will help to open up your understanding and allow you to see many mysteries contained in the Scriptures that some Christians have never experienced. As a matter of record, let me state very emphatically, that no one person has insight into every verse of the Holy Scriptures. This author has only written on subjects he has been privileged with the vision to draw a clear understanding thereof.

FOREWORD

"BIBLICAL STORIES, THE TRUTH IN PERSPECTIVE, WHAT WE SHOULD DO IN HONOR OF GOD", is an inspired writing, intended to be uplifting for all who venture into these pages. The author uses prophetic privilege in these inspired Bible lessons. We all have gifts given to us by the Holy Spirit. We must learn which of the gifts belong to us on an individual basis. The author recognizes the gifts granted to him and has used those gifts to prepare these lessons to help inspire others in the truth of the Bible. Many clergy only use select portions of the Bible in presenting messages to their congregations. Some portions of the Scriptures are never discussed in the church, as if it is taboo to discuss certain parts of the Holy Scriptures for fear of insulting or offending someone with the truth. "The truth shall set you free."

This author believes the Bible, in its entirety, should be presented to the parishioners, to provide them with the complete truth of what is required of us to have life (body) and life everlasting (soul) in heaven with the Holy Master. Equally as importantly, church going people should read and study the Bible for themselves, and allow the Holy Spirit to teach them what they need to know. These lessons will shine new light on some very old teachings. These lessons cover subjects related to geography, the beginning of humanity, family, evil, slavery, and many things in between. Most significantly, these lessons cover making God first, always.

At the time of receiving the inspiration to write this book, the intention was to write on the origins of humankind. However, the Holy Spirit led me in a different direction. This book is a plethora (wealth of information) of stories with deep-seated meaning and roots that run deep into the families of all human beings. Moreover, the main focus of this book is to emphasize God as first, always and forever.

This book is visionary and inspired by the Holy Spirit, to edify and glorify God the Father. 2 Timothy 3:16 says:

"All Scripture is given by inspiration of God, and is profitable for doctrine, for reproof; for correction, for instruction in righteousness:"

All of the words of the Holy Bible are specifically written, the way they are intentionally. By that I mean, word order, punctuation, sentence structure, and paragraph conclusion. Although, the Holy Bible is complete in all we need to know, and without contradiction, the Omniscient God of heaven left room for those, who study the word, by the inspiration of the Holy Spirit, to expound upon the word. Mind you, not to distort the word but to experience the truth of the word. Our pastors and other religious leaders have been endued with that task; even so, many other people have been granted that same privilege from on High.

I know this to be the truth because 2 Timothy 2:15 says:

"Study to shew thyself approved unto God, a workman that needeth not to be ashamed, rightly dividing the word of truth."

In studying the Word of God, you gain special privilege in increased wisdom, knowledge, and understanding. This is not reserved for members of the clergy only. It is for all who study and put God first in all they do. Telling the truth of the Bible will cause blessings to fall down upon you, that you will not be able to contain.

ACKNOWLEDGEMENTS

First, giving honor to God the Father, my Lord and Savior Jesus Christ, under the guidance of the Holy Spirit. Through them, all things are possible.

In recognition to those, who have read in part or discussed varying sections of this book before its completion, thank you for your time and wisdom: Dr. Carl E. Livingston, Mother Doris Coffey Parker and Sister Shirley A. Vance, of whom both have passed on into glory before this book came into print; Minister Stephen R. Jackson, and my dear friend Mr. Trenton Duboris Thomas and Minister Antoinette (Toni) Madison.

THE PROPHET

The word prophet evokes images in our thoughts and minds of Biblical characters of old. Howbeit, what is a prophet? In the Old Testament, the word prophet recognizes those men and women (prophetess') who foretold the things of God to come. Prophets are endued with wisdom, knowledge, and understanding, concerning the things of God. They inspired others for the ministry of God, to increase the number of God's people, and to broaden the importance of God's plan. Many of them could touch and heal, or touch and cause disease to come upon an individual; or they might simply speak into existence a plague or disease process; such as, the curse Elisha placed upon Gehazi in 2 Kings, Chapter 5. They were filled with authority from God to orchestrate oracles and writings for the Holy Bible. They were men and women of God, set on course by God, to do HIS tasks and lay the foundation for all generations. This is not the textbook definition of a prophet; it is the inspired meaning of the word prophet from someone, who has also been endued with great foresight, and inspiration from God.

Are there still prophets today? Some say, no. However, I boldly proclaim, yes! Are they the same as in the days of old? Yes. The difference being, the prophets of old had great responsibility in contributing to the writings and acts recorded in the Holy Bible. They laid the foundation for everyone coming after them to embrace God through the inspired word they received from the Holy Spirit. Prophets of today have a different calling from God. The word is already written, and is not to be changed because it would be akin to changing God. There are two immutable (unchangeable) things that exist, God and that God does not lie. So, in today's world, what is a prophet? In today's world, a prophet is someone endued with special gifts from God, acting under the influence of the Holy Spirit. They possess special insight into the things of God. They have foresight and vision in and about the Word of God. They are directors of vision for directing and leading the people in the right direction on their earthly journey. They see visions telling them what things that are written in the Scriptures, and the correct interpretation thereof, and what things are still to come to fulfillment, as written in the Scriptures. They are men and women, who prophesy over others, and lead the church in growth, both in size of building and in souls coming to Christ.

Even more significantly, a prophet today, is a man or woman, who knows the Word of God, and then, rightly dividing the Word of God for soul saving in Jesus Christ. Moreover, they bring out the true meaning of the Scriptures and present the word to us bringing it to the forefront of our minds in modern times. The prophet or prophetess expounds and expands upon the Word of God, fully explaining the word, in a manner that is clearly understandable to the audience. Additionally, they are filled with vision for all aspects of life: church growth, outreach programs, care of the old, children, widows, and the poor. They stand strongly and boldly before the Throne of Grace, spreading the good news about our Lord and Savior, Jesus Christ. They rebuke false teachings and those, who are in business (preaching) for the money and not for the saving of souls unto life. Simply put, they are under the influence of the Holy Spirit, to the honor and glory of God, for the administration of and up-building of HIS Kingdom.

Are these modern day prophets perfect? Absolutely not! However, they strive and fight each day for the up-building of God's Kingdom. Do they sin? Absolutely, yes! They are no different than the most prolific Scripture writer in the Holy Bible, the apostle Paul. Paul said about himself, "I die daily." Meaning each day, I have to go before my Father in prayer asking forgiveness for my sins. My brothers and sisters in Christ, there are none of us, who sins not. The Scriptures tell us that as matter of fact leaving no room for doubt that we all come short of the glory of God (Rom. 3:23). What we must do is to covet the best gifts (1 Cor. 12:7-11). Those with the gift of prophesy must use that gift to help others in order to increase God's flock. Amen and hallelujah to HIS name.

NOTE

This compelling account, "BIBLICAL STORIES, THE
TRUTH IN PERSPECTIVE, WHAT WE SHOULD
DO IN HONOR OF GOD" enlighteningly connects
the world of the past to the world of the present. The
author meticulously tackles such issues as color, heredity,
oppression, persecution, and other matters of constraint.
It is profound validation of the Word of God, of God's
absolute redemptive power, and God's certain judgment
upon the workers of evil. Highly recommended reading-
ages 7-107.

Doris C. Parker

12/26/07

CLOSING

The lessons in this book will hopefully open your eyes and allow you to see that, we must treat one another with dignity and respect. We are all family and should help one another as much as possible in life. Just imagine what a wonderful world it would be if we all worked together for the betterment and welfare of all people. Above that, we must honor God, our Father, each day of our earthly journey; giving HIM the praise and the glory. Without HIM we perish. Additionally, we must recognize Jesus Christ as Lord, and allow the Holy Spirit to be our guide, our conscience, teacher, and Granter of wisdom, knowledge, and understanding.

Just as God has given us HIS best in Jesus Christ, and in the Holy Spirit, we too should honor HIM with our physical being. Take care of the body God has given to you, and your body will maintain better performance for you. Your outward appearance should have the character of what your spirit of Christ is in your heart. If you don't have material wealth, it is okay, God does not require wealth, HE owns everything. Yet, even without material wealth, there are still things you can do for Christ: your talent, time, service, and having love for all people.

In recognition of the Trinity, all our lives will be made better. Glory to God, hallelujah to HIS name!

2 KINGS
CHAPTER 18

HONOR GOD

KINGDOM BUILDING

This lesson has to do with doing that which is right in the sight of the LORD. Doing evil in the sight of the LORD results in severe punishment toward the leadership and the people they govern. In these Scriptures, the word evil references idol worship. There is a difference in committing evil acts and sinning. For we all sin and come short of the glory of God. Mind you, neither is good for the soul; however, idol worship results in God becoming angry. HIS wrath and vengeance can be swift, strong, and lead to immediate death.

We have all seen in the Holy Scriptures many times, how the Israelites were punished, and sold into slavery multiple times for idol worship. In this section of our study, we will focus on doing that which is right in the sight of the LORD. In the eighteenth chapter of 2 Kings, we find the story of Hezekiah, his kingdom, and what he did to please God. Starting at verse 3,

"And he did that which was right in the sight of the LORD, according to all that David his father did."

Hezekiah loved the LORD as did David his forefather. This verse is an introduction into what the kings of Israel should have been doing all along, trying to please God. David did many wonderful things as king; however, he did not stop the people from performing idolatry. Look at what Hezekiah does in the next verse.

Verse 4: *"He removed the high places, and brake the images, and cut down the groves, and brake in pieces the brasen serpent that Moses had made: for unto those days the children of Israel did burn incense to it: and he called it Nehushtan."*

This thing was very pleasing to God. God has told us repeatedly that, HE is a jealous God. HIS commandments say that we shall have no other god before HIM. In fact, it says in Exodus 34:14, that in addition to calling God, God, and many other names, HE is also called Jealous. This is very significant because it states, HE will not tolerate the worship of any other but HIMSELF.

Verse 5: *"He trusted in the LORD God of Israel; so that after him was none like him among all the kings of Judah, nor any that were before him."*

Hezekiah loved God with all his heart and soul. He did not tolerate the people burning incense to false gods, bowing down to them, paying tribute to them, or any other form of worship to objects made of wood, metal, or stone. He had it all removed and broken to pieces. No other king in all of Judah had a zero tolerance for idol worship. Hezekiah was unlike any other king to reign over Judah.

Verse 6: *"For he clave to the LORD, and departed not from following him, __but kept his commandments__, which the LORD commanded Moses."*

Hezekiah adhered to all the commandments of the LORD. He never departed from following the ordinances of God all the days of his life. This is very important to understand because it leads us to verse seven. We have discussed many of the trials and tribulations the Israelites faced because of their recalcitrant (stubborn, stiffnecked), evil ways. They were punished over and over again for moving away from God. They suffered harsh and cruel slavery. They were tasked with overbearing workloads from sun up to sun down. Yet, repeatedly after repenting to God, having God forgive them and be restored in HIS favor, they would return to evil rebellion in repeating the practice of idol worship.

Verse 7: *"And the LORD was with him; and he prospered whithersoever he went forth: and he rebelled against the king of Assyria, and __served him not__."*

In God, there is victory, always. Not only are we victorious in God, we also prosper in a number of ways; HE takes care of us, HE makes a way out of no way, HE moves your enemies out of the way, and above all, HE assures us of everlasting life in a glorious mansion. A place that has streets of gold, perfect weather, a place where everything we need is provided for us.

As you continue to read the eighteenth chapter of 2 Kings, you will understand how evil almost always leads to destruction. You see, the Israelis, under the leadership of Hoshea, were sold to the Assyrians, into bondage for participating in idol worship. Israel served false gods, while Hezekiah prohibited such practice in Judah.

2 Kings, Chapter 18, is a very important story about why we should always strive to serve God; worship God only; and do the best we can to be obedient unto HIM. HE is KING! At some point in every day of your life, honor God. Amen.

Review Questions:

1. Hezekiah followed in the footsteps of his father:

a. Nehemiah
b. David
c. Solomon

2. Under the leadership of Hezekiah which of the following were destroyed:

a. Images
b. Groves
c. High places
d. Brasen serpent
e. All of the above

3. Who made the brasen image:

a. Moses
b. Hezekiah
c. Solomon

4. The children of Israel were guilty of burning which of the following to idol gods:

a. Clothes
b. Incense
c. Wood

5. Hezekiah was king of which tribe of the Jews:

a. Benjamin
b. Issachar
c. Ephraim
d. Judah

6. Hezekiah did which of the following to the LORD:

a. Transgressed
b. Clave
c. Evil

7. The LORD caused Hezekiah to do what because he followed HIS commandments:

a. Suffer
b. Prosper
c. Be Leprous

8. Which country did Hezekiah rebel against as king:

a. Ethiopia
b. Samaria
c. Assyria

2 CHRONICLES
CHAPTER 4

THE BEST WE CAN OFFER

KINGDOM BUILDING

In this section of reading, we will discuss the importance of giving the best we have to God; prayer, foresight, wisdom, and the intelligence of Solomon. This chapter provides us with the planning and detail involved in the building of the house of God that Solomon is to build. David, Solomon's father, actually had the vision for the house of God; however, God told David not to build the house because of the blood on David's hands.

Let us look first at giving the best to God. In verse 18, we find an abundance of precious metal to be used in the making of the vessels for the worship services. This metal is one of the precious metals used during this time period to represent high value.

*"Thus Solomon made all these vessels in great abundance: for the weight of the brass **could not be found out**."*

This is a phenomenal amount of brass. There is so much brass they were unable to estimate the tonnage. This brass was used to make the lavers (washbowl, caldron), pomegranates (artificial fruit tree), pommels (fountain), pillars with their bases, pots, shovels, and so forth.

Moreover, it was used to make the altar of sacrifice. As significant as this amount of brass is, verses 19-20 are even more striking in the amount of gold collected and used in the making of other vessels to be used in the worship services. Furthermore; verse 22 lets us know that gold was used in abundance in the construction of the house of God.

*"And Solomon made all the vessels that were for the house of God, the golden altar also, and the tables whereon the shewbread was set; Moreover the candlesticks with their lamps, that they should burn after the manner before the oracle, **of pure gold**;"*

Everything that exists in heaven and in earth came from the God of heaven and earth. The message in these verses is, when we give our best to God, HE renders prosperity and a good life back to us in return. Remember, Solomon was made rich beyond measure by God. We, cannot make God rich because HE owns everything; howbeit, in withholding from God, what belongs to God, HE can cause absolute destitution to fall upon us. What we have to do is to, always give to the church, our neighbors, strangers, and so forth. Giving is a fundamental way to receive blessings. Putting God first, combined with giving will cause blessings to come down from heaven in such abundance that you will not be able to contain them all.

We must be willing to share what we have to help someone else. Giving must come freely from the heart, given without reservation, from the heart.

On prayer, in 2 Chronicles 2:7: Solomon determined to build the house of God, is praying for all that is required to accomplish the task at hand. By wisdom, knowledge, understanding, and intelligence, Solomon asks God to send him someone skilled to build the utensils needed in the worship service. For you see, if we ask not, we receive not. God sent Solomon men with the knowledge to make the required instruments for the worship service. These instruments are the best of quality, made by the best possible craftsmen, for the best God- God. Prayer is how we communicate with God. HE already knows our wishes, needs, and desires. HE can and does provide us with what we need every day. Prayer consummates our relationship with God. Solomon being the wisest of the kings, consulted with God about every aspect considered to make the temple pleasing and pleasant to God. We too, must be willing to consult with God in our decision making. HE will fight our battles, guide our steps, make us to prosper, grant us long life, and much more.

The last part in this lesson has to do with the wisdom of Solomon. Solomon is blessed in every aspect of his life because he always put God first. 2 Chronicles, 4:2 and 6, are great testimonials to Solomon's wisdom. Remember, this wisdom is the gift from God to Solomon.

Verse 2, *"Also he made a **molten sea** of ten cubits from brim to brim, round in compass, and five cubits the height thereof; and a line of thirty cubits did compass it round about."*

This is an enormously significant verse with regard to the wisdom, knowledge, understanding, and intelligence, of Solomon. In reading this verse, it seems that this molten sea is a fountain, such as we see in parks, office buildings, and nice hotels. Indeed, it is far from being an object just for viewing pleasure. Certainly, it is beautiful to look upon. Verses 3-5, tell us all of the decorative arrangements used to make this molten sea a spectacular piece of artwork. Verse 6, finally reveals what the molten sea actually is, what its use is, and who it is for.

*"He made also ten lavers, and put five on the right hand, and five on the left, to wash in them: such things as they offered for the burnt offering they washed in them; **but the sea was for the priests to wash in**."*

This molten sea is a large tub similar to what we today call a bathtub. Why is this significant? By the Omniscient God of heaven, Solomon received the knowledge for indoor plumbing. The priests would slaughter the animals for sacrifice and wash them in the lavers, in preparation for the ceremony of worship. After the animals were cleaned, the priests would have to also clean themselves before the ceremony was to commence.

This molten sea held ten thousand baths, a huge amount of water. They used a system of what we call plumbing to fill this huge bath tub. Furthermore, there was a system for heating the water flowing into the molten sea. Did you know that many centuries ago there was actually indoor plumbing and a system for heating the water? The priest would clean themselves in heated water that was pumped into the temple

In giving back to God, give freely from the heart. Smile as in cheer when giving. Give what you can without causing a burden for you and your family, otherwise, your giving could later lead to regret of giving, thereby voiding the blessing of giving. Above all else, give God the glory, and the honor everyday. Praise HIM, praise HIM, praise HIM. Amen.

Review Questions:

1. Solomon made the vessels for worship in great abundance:

a. True
b. False

2. The vessels for worship were made of silver and gold:

a. True
b. False

3. The weight of the brass used in making the vessels is pounds is:

a. 5,000
b. 10,000
c. 20,000
d. Unknown

4. The golden altar was made of:

a. Half gold
b. One forth gold
c. Pure gold

5. Golden candlesticks were a part of the worship ceremony:

a. True
b. False

6. The molten sea was a place to wash the animals to be offered for sacrifice:

a. True
b. False

7. The lavers were for the priests to wash in:

a. True
b. False

PRAY TOWARD HEAVEN

KINGDOM BUILDING

Pray toward heaven. In this chapter, we will discuss prayer, as demonstrated in the words of the most wise king of all time, Solomon. After Solomon had completed building the house of God, he prayed a heart felt and sincere prayer to God. From verses 20 to 38, Solomon uses the word *"toward"* six times in reference to praying to God. Solomon also uses the words *"spread forth hands."* There is even mention of God's 'stretched out arm.' There is a tremendous lesson about prayer in this chapter.

Starting with verse 18, after the house of God was completed, Solomon knew that no matter how great a house he has built, that God is everywhere and that heaven above cannot contain HIM. Solomon's prayer more or less was stating to God, my hope, my wish, and my desire LORD, is that I have done work in building this house that is pleasing unto YOU, Father; that this work is acceptable in THY sight.

In verses 20 and 21 come the first two, *"toward this place."* These verses are a prelude into the rest of the chapter. The first, *"toward this place"* is essentially saying, when the people pray, let them pray facing toward the house of

God, paying tribute to that which is representative of the perfection of God. The second, *"toward this place"* says, as YOU look down on this people, praying to YOU, looking toward a physical similitude of YOUR design, hear them though YOU are in heaven above.

Verses 21 and 26 use the words, *"toward this place"* in asking the people to face the house of God, when praying for forgiveness when they commit sin.

Verse 29 is telling us that God honors us lifting our hands in prayer, praise, and in worshiping HIM. If we don't praise HIM the rocks will cry out for us. When the people are in the sanctuary worshiping God, all arms should be raised and stretched forth giving God all the honor, all the praise, and all of the glory.

Let's examine verse 29 in its entirety, *"Then what prayer or what supplication soever shall be made of any man, or of all thy people Israel, when every one shall know his own sore and his own grief, and shall __spread forth his hands in this house__:"*

In other words, for whatever reason this person is praying, whether for sinning, grief, or whatever the cause, let him lift his hands and stretch them forth to the honor and glory of God, in the house of God. The reasoning behind this piece of Scripture is this, when we are in God's house of prayer, some are ashamed or embarrassed to make a sound or to raise their hands in the presence of others. This Scripture is not only saying is it okay to do those things; conjunctively, it is saying, we should do those things. God loves everything we do to honor HIM. HE created us for the sole purpose of worshiping HIM.

Now look at this. Not only should we pray toward heaven and lift our arms toward heaven in honor to God, God HIMSELF, stretches forth HIS arms in receipt of our prayers. Hear the words in verse 32:

*"Moreover concerning the stranger, which is not of thy people Israel, but is come from a far country for thy great name's sake, and thy mighty hand, and **thy stretched out arm**; if they come and pray in this house;"*

This is a phenomenal verse. It is sender and Receiver. We stretch forth our arms to the Father, sending HIM our request or supplication, and HE, as the Grantor of prayer requests, stretches forth HIS arms to receive and process the request. The other good news is, it does not matter if you are Jew or Gentile, as long as you are giving God the honor and the glory, recognizing HIM as Supreme. Halleluiah, praise God.

Now listen to the words in verse 33. What an awesome God we serve. If we are faithful to do what HE has told us to do in honoring HIM, HE listens to the message, processes the request, and grants the wish.

Verse 33, *"Then hear thou from the heavens, even from thy dwelling place, and do according to all that the <u>stranger calleth to thee for</u>; that <u>all people</u> of the earth may <u>know thy name</u>, and fear thee, as doth thy people Israel, and may know that this house which I have built is called by thy name."*

This is an absolutely remarkable verse. For you see, the Jews have been granted special status as the chosen people of God. Inasmuch, it does not matter if you are Jew or Gentile, as long as you recognize God as Supreme. It does not matter what country you come from, what your ethnicity is, what language you speak. God loves the praises of all people and HE is an impartial God. Yes, the Jews were chosen as God's people; however, it was not intended for anyone to think that being Jew makes them the only people, whom God would accept and recognize. The purpose of choosing a particular group of people was this, everything has to be in order. The Jews were chosen to be the directors of what all people need to do to be pleasing and acceptable in the sight of God. The Jews were to be the example for other peoples to follow in worship, praise, and in giving honor to God.

Reach out for God and HE will extend HIS hand out to you. This is Bible country. Give God the honor each and everyday of your life. In the name of Jesus, Amen.

Review Questions:

1. When praying in the house of God, we should?

a. Fold our arms across one another
b. Hold our hands behind our backs
c. Stretch forth our arms in the temple

2. God listens to the prayers of all people who honor and obey HIM?

a. True
b. False

3. When we pray with stretched out arms to God, HE stretches forth HIS hands to receive our request?

a. True
b. False

4. The house that Solomon built is called by what name?

a. The house of God
b. The temple of God
c. The sanctuary of God

2 CHRONICLES
CHAPTER 7

TO PRAISE OR TO FORSAKE

KINGDOM BUILDING

To praise or to forsake. There is one rule that comes from God that should always be observed in our daily lives. This rule has multiple segments to it, which are completely related to one another, and intertwined like the blood flowing through our veins is present throughout our bodies. It is the rule that pertains to the commandments of God: We shall have no other gods before HIM. We shall not make any graven image of anything in heaven above or in earth beneath. We shall not bow down to any false gods or serve any false gods; and we shall not take the name of the LORD, our God in vain (Deuteronomy, Chapter 5).

This chapter of Chronicles relates to Solomon and the words of God given to him after the completion of the house of God. This visitation from God to Solomon comes after Solomon's prayer to God with regard to what Solomon prays for in Chapter 6. God's response begins at verse 7:12,

"And the LORD appeared to Solomon by night, and said unto him, I have heard thy prayer, and have chosen this place to myself for an house of sacrifice."

This verse is a testament to the wisdom and knowledge God gave to Solomon. In effect, this verse says, I totally accept this temple that you have built in MY honor. It is beautiful and made of the best materials available to you. You have done your best and given the best to make this place pleasing unto ME; therefore, I accept the work of your hands.

Verses 14-16, tell us to honor God always, to turn away from evil, and HE will hear our prayers from heaven. HIS instructions are simple, pray in this place, the place that I have chosen to put MY name there, and I will forgive your sins. Verses 17-18 are specific to Solomon and to the linage that Solomon is a part of, the linage that the kings to rule Israel are to come from. All of this is about God being pleased with Solomon and the house that Solomon built.

Solomon gives God the best that he can offer. Today, God is still pleased with us giving HIM the best that we can. Praise and worship, honor and glory, singing and shouting, lifting our hands to HIM in the house of worship. We must give God all the hallelujahs we can muster up. HE loves the praises of HIS people. Remember, HE created us to worship HIM, HE loves the praises of HIS people.

Now let us examine the rest of this chapter. Because God loves all of the praises; and because HE is a jealous God; HIS punishment for those, who turn away from giving HIM the praise, the honor, and the glory, can be very harsh and without mercy. While we all sin, we must never apostatize (turn away) from God. HIS forgiveness for sin is endless; however, HE has absolutely no tolerance for evil doing (witchcraft, observing of times, enchantments, familiar spirits, wizards, idolatry, etc.) (2 Kings 21:6). Starting at verse 20, this chapter takes on a different kind of message for the Israelites. This warning uses strong words from God, and the message is clear to anyone reading this Scripture.

Verse 20, *"Then will I pluck them up by the roots out of **my land** which I have given them; and this house, which I have sanctified for my name, will I cast out of my sight, and will make it to be a proverb and a byword among all nations."*

Warning, warning, the Jealous God of heaven will strike with great vengeance upon this, MY people, if they turn away from ME. I will make a mockery of them for making a mockery of ME. You will become a proverb (prisoner, compress, afflict) and a byword (point, taunt), by all the world. I will put you out of my land that I have given to you. I will not look down from heaven upon you any longer with favor. You will be punished by, imprisoned by, and taunted by all the nations of the world. This is an awful punishment. God does not want to punish us; however, HE will for transgressing into idolatry and breaking the commandments. It is our punishment for moving away from God. Break the curse. Come back to God and break the curse. HE is waiting on you.

Verses 21-22 bring the point home, *"And this house, which is high, shall be an **astonishment** to every one that passeth by it; so that he shall say, Why hath the LORD done thus unto this land, and unto this house? And it shall be answered, **Because they forsook the LORD God** of their fathers, which brought them forth out of the land of Egypt, and laid hold on other gods, and <u>worshipped them,</u> and <u>served them</u>: therefore hath he brought all this evil upon them."*

In other words, the house that Solomon built will be ruins. It will be in such a horrible state of disrepair, that when men see it, they will question what happened to this beautiful house of worship. Why has the LORD destroyed a place that was built in HIS honor? The answer is, "...THEY FORSOOK THE LORD GOD..."

Folks, the most ruinous mistake anyone can make is to turn away from God. The Israelites forsook God even after they had been shown over and over again HIS might, HIS power, and what HE would do to them for transgressing. Transgression equals curse; obedience and putting HIM first equals blessings. Reexamine the history of the Israelites, we have looked at thus far in our lessons. The books of Kings and of Chronicles tell it all. Time after time the Israelites would be compliant to the will of God and then apostatize from God. In every instance, they were punished for moving away from HIM. In every instance of serving HIM, they were blessed. The solution to being blessed is a simple one, serve God only. It is a simple but profound statement. HE has to be the only God in your life, Amen!

In light of the above Scriptures, one might assume an attitude that all is lost. It does not matter what they do, their status will remain blighted because of the oppressive society we live in. Hold up! There is a cure. Yes, we may face oppression all of the days of our earthly journey; however, if you turn to God, HE will move your enemies out of the way. You will have some trials and tribulations but victory is assured in the name of our Lord and Savior Jesus Christ. Let me tell you, I face prejudice and bigotry on my job almost daily. I don't let it get me down because I know that what God has for me is for me. I am blessed beyond measure, not in material things, though God has provided well for me; but rather, in health, food, clothing, shelter, job, transportation, family, and much more. You see, while I am imperfect, I know that God is first in my life; the sacrificial blood of Jesus cleanses my sins daily. Paul said, 'I die daily.' In other words, I ask forgiveness for my sins everyday. There is no man that sinneth not. What I am trying to convey is this, when you return to God, and break the curse of generational degradation, there are still going to be problems that will come your way. As a Christian, Satan is always coming for you, roaming the earth seeking whom, he can devour (1 Peter 5:8). This pertains to Christians. Satan does not go about seeking to devour that which is already his. It is the Christian, he is trying to make fall in order to build his kingdom.

It is up to you to praise or to forsake God. You and your family can be made whole by following The One and Only True and Living God. Make the best choice. It is the only choice. Break the curse.

Praise God daily in the name of Jesus. Amen.

Review Questions:

1. God called the house that Solomon built a house of:

a. Sacrifice
b. House of praise
c. Place of worship

2. God appeared to Solomon in the night:

a. True
b. False

3. The house that Solomon built was sanctified by God:

a. True
b. False

4. God said HE would pluck the children of Israel from:

a. The house Jealousy
b. The house of Greed
c. Other nations

5. God promised to make the house that Solomon built
    a _____ if the people turned away from HIM:

a. Embarrassment
b. Astonishment
c. Palace

6. The house that Solomon built will be destroyed if the children of Israel do what:

a. Forsake the LORD God
b. Worship God
c. Fight amongst themselves

BEAUTIFUL HOUSE
OF WORSHIP

KINGDOM BUILDING

Keeping God's house in order. We have a duty and an obligation to God to keep HIS house looking as beautiful and clean as humanly possible. God gives the best, Jesus Christ, and expects only the best from us to HIM. Moreover, HE requires the best we have to offer to HIM, us.

Verse 5, *"And he gathered together the priests and the Levites, and said to them, Go out unto the cities of Judah, and gather of all Israel money to repair the house of your God from year to year, and see that ye hasten the matter. Howbeit the Levites hastened it not."*

During the reign of kings Jehoram and Ahaziah, much evil was wrought in Israel. There were murders and all manner of sin going on that both kings allowed under their watch. As a result, great torment came upon the people, great plagues to smite the people, young and old, men and women. Even their personal possessions were plagued. This is all found in 2 Chronicles, Chapters 20-21. More significantly, these kings allowed fornication (whoring, idol worship) to be practiced during their reign.

That led to the house that Solomon built being left to decay and become ruins. These are not the only kings, who did evil in the sight of the LORD. Rehoboam did evil as well. Under his reign the treasures of the house of the LORD and of the king's house were removed (2 Chronicles, Chapter 12). Through at least three kings, evil has flourished, and The One and Only True and Living God, has been denied. That led to the house that Solomon built receiving no attention and falling into a desperate state of disrepair.

The above Scripture is representative of a new beginning in Israel. Joash is now king and his plan is to do that which is right in the sight of the LORD. He is commanding the priests and the Levites to collect money from all, who are willing to give, to restore the house that Solomon built. This is not a one time order, it is to be done every year for the upkeep of God's house. Joash requested they do this with hast; however, the Levites did not act on the king's order to quickly begin collecting the money needed for the restoration of the temple.

The point of the verse is this; God's house must be maintained in glorious fashion. Not only should we make the house of God beautiful, it should be spectacularly beautiful. It should be ornate, opulent, brilliantly lighted with silver and gold decorations. There should not be a more splendid building anywhere, before the church. We have an obligation to see to it that of the money collected during worship service, that just as a portion should go to helping those in need, taking care of the head of the church, paying the musician, etcetera, is that a portion should always go toward keeping the church beautiful and clean.

In verses 6-10, the Levites continued to disobey the order of the king, howbeit, the king is intelligent and approached the matter from a different direction. He made a proclamation throughout the country that excited the people. The king had a chest made and placed it at the entering in of the house of the LORD. Look at verse 11.

"Now it came to pass, that at what time the chest was brought unto the king's office by the hand of the Levites, and when they saw that there was much money, the king's scribe and the high priest's officer came and emptied the chest, and took it, and carried it to his place again. Thus they did day by day, and gathered money in abundance."

This is particularly interesting to discuss. The Levites built this chest and placed it where the king told them to put it. As the people passed by, they would cast into the chest until there was much money in the chest. Now get this, the Levites, who were supposed to be over the collection, who were unwilling to collect the money, as commanded by the king, still don't get the money. The money was collected by the scribe (recorder) and the chief (head priest). The people cast so much money into the chest that the chest had to be emptied over and over again, day by day.

Verse 12, *"And the king and Jehoiada gave it to such as did the work of the service of the house of the LORD, and hired masons and carpenters to repair the house of the LORD, and also such as wrought iron and brass to mend the house of the LORD."*

The king and Jehoiada collected the money and hired the best skilled laborers possible to do the work on the sanctuary. These men were skilled in all manner of crafts: iron, brass, carpentry, and brick masonry. Though not named, they also hired those skilled in sculpting and in glass working. How do I know this to be true? Verse 13 tells me so. These men restored the house of God from bottom to top, and from left to right. Every aspect of the temple was restored to brilliant glory, worthy of the honor of God.

Verse 13, *"So the workmen wrought and the work was perfected by them, and they set the house of God in his state, and strengthened it."*

Not only did they restore the house of God, they improved it. Here is the key factor about these verses, the work that these men did was done to perfection. My fellow believers, this is the only way it should be done. When giving to God, do the best for HIM that you can. HE loves it! Individually, we may never do such a great work as building a church but that does not matter. As insignificant a work as you may believe you are involved in, in service to God, it is not insignificant to God. You see, in addition to God loving the praises of HIS people, HE also loves our service in honor to HIM. Your part in the church may be to clean or to prepare meals. What ever your role in the church is, do it to the best of your ability. It is a part of your Christian duty, and HE recognizes your work just as HE recognizes the work of the man of God, the pastor.

In closing this lesson on keeping God's house in order, let me caution you on being critical about the cost of decorating and maintaining God's house. If you believe that opulence and splendor, with great price tags are over doing it, remember this, it is all HIS anyway. Furthermore, HE gave us HIS only Begotten Son for our salvation, the best gift of all. HE loves us! Yes, we must be prudent in our spending, but if the item is not over priced, don't make an issue about spending for God. Trying to do things cheaply that pertain to God, could cause you to lose your blessings. And, I must say this, if the members of the church are driving around in fine, expensive automobiles, and the house of worship is not decorated well, or the building is in need of repair, perhaps those members are more materialistic than Christian. We must have our priorities in order.

God is Perfection. Give to keep HIS house in order, and HE will reward you in your efforts. Glory to Your name Father. Amen.

Review Questions:

1. Joash gathered which of these people together to collect the money for rebuilding the church:

a. Israelites
b. Priests
c. Levites
d. B and C

2. The Levites immediately followed the commandment of the king:

a. True
b. False

3. King Joash had what built to collect the money therein:

a. Chest
b. Collection plate
c. Basket

4. The Scribe and the high priest officer emptied the money day by day:

a. True
b. False

5. There was only a small amount of money collected in the chest each day:

a. True
b. False

6. The work done by the workers was done perfectly:

a. True
b. False

7. The house of God was made stronger than it was originally:

a. True
b. False

JOB
CHAPTERS 1-42

A MAN OF GREAT FAITH

KINGDOM BUILDING

A righteous man of great honor, dignity, respect, and above all, a great man of God. The Book of Job reads like a great court trial of bantering back and forth between the prosecution and the defense. The arguments presented by both sides are strong and persuasive in their justifications. Before these arguments ensued, the Holy Bible gives us an overview of Job to provide us with a clear picture of the God fearing man Job is. Verse 1 reads:

*"THERE was a man in the land of Uz, whose name was Job; and that man was **perfect and upright**, and one that **feared God**, and eschewed evil."*

Job possessed a good heart, full of righteousness, and the love of God. He had a strong displeasure for evil: eschew-to stay away from, to decline, to depart from, to remove. Job avoided all evil and did not allow anyone to practice evil around him. Because of his commitment to God, God blessed him abundantly in houses, livestock, riches, and family. In fact, Job was so upright that Satan, who was going to and fro on the earth seeking whom he may devour, that God said to Satan in verse 1:8,

*"And the LORD said unto Satan, Hast thou considered my servant Job, that there is none like him in the earth, **a perfect and an upright man**, one that feareth God, and escheweth evil?"*

What praise from God about a man, perfect and upright! What an honor for Job, praise befitting a deity from God, The One and Only True Deity, giving praise for a flesh and blood being. Satan is bold in his response to God about Job, and asked for the hedge of protection around Job to be removed, in order for Satan to make his attack on Job. Let me state emphatically, no one can entice God to do anything. God did remove the hedge of protection from Job; however, HE did not do it for Satan, HE did it to show that Job is truly a God fearing man.

With the hedge of protection removed, with all of his power still intact that he had in heaven Satan attacked. Don't be fooled about the power of Satan. There is no mention in the Scriptures anywhere about Lucifer's power being taken away when he became Satan. Satan began his attack on Job. He destroyed all of Job's livestock, and killed all of his children. Can you imagine the stress and heartbreak Job was going through? Yet, in all his lamenting and grief, Job continued in his righteousness toward God. Verse 1:22 reads:

"In all this Job sinned not, nor charged God foolishly."

When Satan spoke to God initially about Job and God responded, HE told Satan not to put his hands on Job's person. After Satan brought destructive forces upon Job and did not achieve the results he was looking for, Satan had another conversation with God about Job. This time Satan was given permission to afflict Job's personage, short of taking his life. Satan went on the attack again striking Job with sores and boils from the top of his head to the soles of his feet. In verses 2:4-6, we find the reasoning Satan uses to justify afflicting Job's flesh. Satan had thought that would be enough to cause Job to lose his faith and trust in God. Poor Job was infested with draining wounds all over his body, yet he did not give up on being righteous.

Then came Eliphaz, Bildad, and Zophar, Job's friends. They were very distraught about Job's condition. He was so severely disfigured that initially they did not recognize him. They all tore their clothing and threw dust upon their heads, as was common practice for any devastating or tragic event during those times. Job gave them a speech in Chapter 3 that reads like a pity party for his life. The first one to respond to Job was Eliphaz in Chapter 4. His rebuttal to Job begins the bantering between all of these men. Eliphaz was convinced that Job had done something to bring all of this destruction upon him.

After Eliphaz presented his rhetoric to Job, Job countered with his desire to die because death would be better than the awful torment he is enduring. The bantering goes on between Job, Eliphaz, Bildad, and Zophar, for many chapters. In Chapter 27, verse 4, Job says:

"My lips shall not speak wickedness, nor my tongue utter deceit."

The good news in this is, Job never gave up on God and continued to fear The One and Only True and Living God. Job's plight did not change his faith. The devil is a liar! Satan had convinced himself that Job would curse God to HIS face if he brought all this destruction upon him. The point in this is, no matter what your situation is you must still make God your number one priority. Nothing but nothing can come before God. No matter how down and out you are, no matter what misfortune has plagued you, no matter how down in the mire you are, give it over to God and HE will rescue you from yourself, and the grip that Satan has on you.

God listened to all of the bantering between these men and in Chapters 38-41, HE responds to all of the charges and rebuttals. HE tells them that everything is under HIS control. You see, the wild beasts of the field, the fowl of the air, creatures of the water, are all subject to the God of the heavens. Get this, even the wind, the rain, the earth, the sun and the moon obey God. The day and the night obey. The planets and galaxies recognize and obey God. How much more should we, who are created in HIS likeness, in HIS image, obey? Job never gave up on God. We too, must possess that same spirit of making and keeping God first in our lives. HE will reward you openly for worshipping HIM.

Eliphaz, Bildad, and Zophar, could have been severely punished for all of the allegations they brought against the man of God. In Chapter 42, verse 7, the LORD says,

"And it was so, that after the LORD had spoken these words unto Job, the LORD said to Eliphaz the Temanite, My ***wrath*** *is kindled against thee, and against thy two friends: for ye have not spoken of me the thing that is right, as my servant Job hath."*

God was not pleased with these men and told them to go before Job and to have Job pray for them and for them to offer up sacrifices for their trespasses. The point cannot be emphasized more my Christian friends, DO NOT PUT YOUR MOUTH ON THE MAN OF GOD. You will lose!

Job had endured an awful burden; he lost all that he had, including all of his children. But, oh, by the greatness of God, look at what happened in verses 42:10-13,

"And the LORD turned the ***captivity of Job***, *when he prayed for his friends: also the LORD gave Job twice as much as he had before. 11 Then came there unto him all his brethren, and all his sisters, and all they that had been of his acquaintance before, and did eat bread with him in his house: and they bemoaned him, and comforted him over all the evil that the*

LORD had brought upon him: <u>every man also gave him a</u> <u>*piece of* **money**, *and every one an* **earring of gold**</u>. *12 So the LORD blessed the latter end of Job more than his beginning: for he had fourteen thousand sheep, and six thousand camels, and a thousand yoke of oxen, and a thousand she asses. 13 He had also seven sons and three daughters."*

These verses are very important. Inasmuch, because Job continued in faith to God, God loosed him from the bonds of Satan. Satan had Job's body but not his spirit. Once Job proved by praying for his friends that he is a man of God, God removed Job from Satan's grip, and restored the hedge of protection around Job. God then openly blessed Job and gave him more than Satan had taken away. Here is another striking point in these verses; some might believe that times of trouble come from the LORD. In fact, times of trouble will always come your way when you are in the LORD. Satan is always out seeking which child of God, he can devour. Satan does not have to go after that which already belongs to him; he is seeking to destroy those who fear the LORD, trying to build his kingdom. Don't get thrown down and trapped by the subtilty and beguiling deception of Satan. Those, who are not in the LORD, bring their on destruction with them everywhere they go. They don't understand why every thing they touch is like a pile of dung. It is because they don't have God in their life.

These verses are rich in much significant advice for us. Here is another point; look at what the people did for the man of God. They presented him with an abundance of gifts. Do you support your pastor, the man of God? You should! He is the representative of God.

Is he doing the work appointed him from God? Again, the emphasis must be made, he is a man, don't expect perfection, as Job is. However, everything must be done in order and respectfully. He cannot be indecent and out of order, a public embarrassment.

Lastly, in these verses, for those who believe men should not wear earrings, men have worn earrings from early Bible days. Look at Exodus 32:2, the people were told to give up their earrings, the wives, daughters, and their sons. Mind you, the reason they gave their earrings was abominable, that is not the issue. The point being there is nothing wrong with males having earrings.

The Book of Job is a very valuable book for all of us. It tells us that putting God first is the best decision we can ever make. In coming to the end of this lesson, we have to turn back to Job, Chapter 2. You see, the Bible refers to the woman as the weaker vessel. Job makes a great case for this saying. Repeatedly, throughout these lessons, we have heard there is a specific order to everything. The weaker vessel comes into play because the man came before the woman. Job had lost everything; he was afflicted with sores and boils all over his body. He was severely grieved to the point of wishing he would die, or even more strikingly, that he had presented from his mother's womb still born.

Job's wife came to him and said in verse 2:9,

"… Dost thou still retain thine integrity? curse God, and die."

Job could not believe his ears. Can you imagine the way he must have looked at her as he spoke these words in verse 10,

"… Thou speakest as one of the foolish women speaketh. What? shall we receive good at the hand of God, and shall we not receive evil? In all this did not Job sin with his lips."

What more foolish and unwise advice could have been proposed to a man, who was already suffering tremendous turmoil. Had Job listened to her, surely he would have become the property of Satan. From studying the Holy Scriptures, by count, this is the fourth time in the Scriptures, a woman, has advised a man in an unwise and foolish manner. Ecclesiastes 7:26 says,

*"And I find **more bitter than death the woman**, whose heart is snares and nets, and her hands as bands: **whoso pleaseth God shall escape from her**; but the **sinner shall be** taken by her."*

The fact is, a woman, the weaker vessel, who is not virtuous, is a trap waiting to be filled by an unwise man. Not to defame women because the Holy Bible also says, a man that finds a wife, finds a good thing. However, a woman with malice in her heart is a fatal instrument to the unwise man. This verse says, it is better to die than to fall into the hands of a bitter woman. If the man is not prayed up and in fear of the LORD, he will make vital and critical errors in judgment listening to the foolish woman, who is not virtuous.

The Book of Job tells us to always keep God first in our lives. It is a testimony to the benefits of living righteously. This book tells us that all, who come to us with advice, may not have our best interest at heart. Concurrently, it tells us that a man must be wise, allowing the Holy Spirit to govern his decisions; and not allow the love of his life, his wife, to give him bad advice. Moreover, for him not to follow bad advice that could lead to greater destruction.

Keep God first always (Mat 6:33), and HE will take care of you. Amen.

Review Questions:

1. Job was an upright and perfect man:

a. True
b. False

2. Job practiced faithfully before God and eschewed evil:

a. True
b. False

3. After Job was attacked by Satan and lost everything, including his children, Job sinned against God:

a. True
b. False

4. Job became bitter and spoke evil and deceit in time of trouble:

a. True
b. False

5. What did God tell Eliphaz, Bildad, and Zophar, about the things they said in bantering with Job:

a. That HE was pleased with them
b. That they are all well spoken
c. That HIS wrath is kindled against them

EVIL GAIN, ONLY TO LOSE

KINGDOM BUILDING

Will you stand up for right and do good, or partake of evil devices unto your own hurt? We have choices in life as to where life will take us. This lesson is about serving God, doing good, uncontrolled anger, and keeping away from evil. The opening verses to this chapter are a powerful message concerning God taking care of HIS people and the evildoers.

Psalm 37:1-4, *"FRET not thyself because of evildoers, neither be thou envious against the workers of iniquity. 2 For they shall soon be cut down like the grass, and wither as the green herb. 3 Trust in the LORD, and do good; so shalt thou dwell in the land, and verily thou shalt be fed. 4 Delight thyself also in the LORD; and he shall give thee the desires of thine heart."*

Glory to God, Hallelujah to HIS name. These verses are full of the richness that all are entitled too, by living righteously, or to the destruction of those, who choose to live unrighteously. As God fearing people, never envy those who have obtained riches by cunning and deceiving methods. They have their reward. As a child of God, HE will provide all that you need. Let me tell you, I am blessed, blessed, and more blessed. No, I am not rich, but I am living large. Don't get me wrong. I am not boasting, just stating the truth. I put God first, always. HE in turn provides well for me. Yes, I have material things; they are gifts from my Father, just as parents give gifts to their children. I am a child of God. What we must do is to stay away from evil behaviors. This is not about sin; we all sin and come short of the glory of God. This is about doing that which you consciously conceive and contrive that causes harm to someone else. Even more so, it is about not making God the first priority in your life. HE must come first.

Verses 8-9, very importantly is an area that most of us can use a little help with. It is okay to have anger; however, swift anger overrides good judgment.

"Cease from anger, and forsake wrath: fret not thyself in any wise to do evil. 9 For evildoers shall be cut off: but those that wait upon the LORD, they shall inherit the earth."

Wrath belongs to the LORD. We must never seek to take revenge for wrongs other have perpetrated upon us. To be matter of fact, if we seek to get even with others for their wrongs, we are wrong. This is evil behavior. Let go and let God. I can remember many times in my life when I thought to get even with someone because of the pain and hurt they caused me. However, there was always a little voice telling me, no. Swift anger or overwhelming anger (wrath) will lead to nothing but destruction. It is this intense anger that leads to envy, jealousy, murder, sabotage, and much more. If we resolve to engage in these types of behavior, God will cause us to *"wither as the green herb."* Allow yourself to flourish by turning it over to God.

The good news is this. We all deserve death because of the sin in us. Howbeit, God, WHO, created us, knows that after the fall of man that we all have sin born in us. Yes, sin does trouble HIM, but because of the love HE has for us, HE forgives our sin. Evil on the other hand, is something that can cause immediate death and possibly eternal damnation. Verses 23-24, read:

*"The steps of a good man are ordered by the LORD: and he delighteth in his way. 24 **Though he fall**, he shall not be utterly cast down: for the LORD **upholdeth him with his hand**."*

Glory to the Father. Amen. This is amazing testimony to the goodness of God and the love HE has for us. A good man has a conscience that prevents him from going too far to the left or right. This is of the Spirit that comes from God. In keeping God first and in staying away from evil, God will guide you the rest of the way. Now get this, though you keep God first, you still have a part of you that may cause you to commit sin. This may even be a daily occurrence. We all fall down. The good news is, get back up again. HE will not destroy you because you fell down; however, HE expects you to stand upon your feet and not stay down. Look closely at these verses, not only do you need to get back up again, in doing so, HE will reach down to help you up.

Verses 37-40, go on to tell us that those who try to live righteously will have peace, salvation, and HIS help, even in time of trouble. The most important thing we can do is to put God first, always. Putting our trust in HIM will render rewards beyond your highest wishes and desires. Don't let evil behaviors rend you of the blessings of God, and lead your soul to destruction.

Give God some of your time every day. It is the least that we should do. Glory to HIS mane. Amen.

Review Questions:

1. Evil doers are to be envied because of the wealth they obtain in life:

a. True
b. False

2. To be cut down as the grass, or to wither away like the green herb is the reward of evildoers:

a. True
b. False

3. To delight thyself in the LORD, HE will give you the desires of your heart:

a. True
b. False

4. Anger and wrath are evil behaviors that lead to salvation:

a. True
b. False

5. Those, who wait upon the LORD, shall inherit the earth:

a. True
b. False

6. The steps of an unrighteous man are ordered by the LORD:

a. True
b. False

7. Though a man put God first, he will be cast down and utterly destroyed when he falls down:

a. True
b. False

CREATURES OF GOD'S LOVE

KINGDOM BUILDING

To dwell in the house of the LORD. God takes care of all HIS creatures. Man, the only one of God's creations to have a soul, is the highest living being in the sight of God. Yet, HE cares for all HIS creatures from the lowest form of life, upward. From the smallest living creature, to the largest, to the most revered, humankind. In verse 3, it says,

"Yea, the sparrow hath found an house, and the swallow a nest for herself, where she may lay her young, even thine alters, O LORD of hosts, my King, and my God."

In as much as God has made a way for all of us to be provided for, HE has always provided a means for the simplest of animals and even the fowls of the air to be provided for as well. God takes care of HIS own. The difference between the fowls of the air, animals, and humans is this; man is the only creature with a living soul. This brings us to verse 4,

"Blessed are they that dwell in thy house: they will be still praising thee. Selah."

You see, no matter what creature it is, it is of God and made by God. HE has provided a way for all of his creatures to have housing. Man has another house, a house not made by hands. A house to live in forevermore; a great temple with many rooms, a place where our souls will live forever and always. In that house, we will be praising our Creator all the day long. Start praising and worshipping HIM now, on your earthly journey. This is our practice field. We only get one trip through our earthly existence.

Look at how much more value (Selah) our heavenly existence holds than our earthly journey. Verse 10 says,

"For a day in thy courts is better than a thousand, I had rather be a doorkeeper in the house of my God, than to dwell in the tents of wickedness."

This is a very profound statement. One day in heaven is better than a thousand days of living on earth. It is better to hold any position in heaven than to be the most notable person on earth. I don't know about you, but I would rather live in heaven, with my Father, as a janitor, than to live in the most lavish home on earth, with all of the luxuries that money can buy. The good news is, it is simple to achieve this goal. Verse 11 tells us that God will provide everything we need. HE is our Sun, our Protector, our All in All. What we have to do is make HIM our number One. Living righteously, forsaking evil, and making HIM first in our lives. In doing so nothing will be withheld from us. Don't get me wrong in this.

Even the strongest Christian will have trials, troubles, sorrows, and pains, during their journey of our earthly travel. However, in death all things are ours. Nothing in heaven will be withheld from us. We will talk to The Trinity and be in Their presence 24/7. Amen.

Verse 12 sums it up:

"O LORD of hosts, blessed is the man that trusteth in thee."

By trusting in the LORD, all things are possible. In trust, HE reigns Supreme. In trust, HE is always first in your life. In trust, salvation is obtained. In trust, all worry and despair vanish away. In trust, you are heaven bound. Amen.

Review Questions:

1. God, our Creator, has made a way for all of HIS creatures to have housing:

a. True
b. False

2. In heaven we will be praising God forever:

a. True
b. False

3. What number represents in earthly time a day in heaven:

a. 100
b. 10
c. 1000

4. One day in heaven is better than any length of time on earth:

a. True
b. False

5. Trusting in the LORD results in blessings on earth:

a. True
b. False

LIVING UNGODLY

KINGDOM BUILDING

Of sin, of iniquity, and of transgression. These are titles that cover a multitude of ungodly behaviors, whether of the body or of the mind, moreover, of the soul. This chapter of Psalms starts off telling us what we should do in order to be pleasing to God. It is a prayer of blessing to the LORD.

"BLESS the LORD, O my soul: and all that is within me, bless his holy name. Bless the LORD, O my soul, and forget not all his benefits:"

Blessing God brings blessings or rewards back to us in great abundance. Blessing the LORD causes every aspect of our lives to improve, including the revival of our spirit. These two verses have several aspects of great life built into them. The first being, to give honor to God, as our first priority. This in turn leads to our own soul being blessed by God for putting HIM in HIS proper place, first. The next reward in these two verses speaks of benefits for the soul. These benefits are multifaceted, covering the soul, the flesh, disease processes, eternal life, and the love God has for us, and all of that combined with the mercy HE also has for us.

All of this is about the goodness we are to direct toward God, and the promises of such an act toward us: goodness returned to us from HIM. There will never be more blessings in your life that can be reaped than keeping God as your number one priority. HE is Supreme. HIS name is Jealous. No one, nothing, is to come before HIM. Honor HIM daily, no matter what your day is like. In fact, when your day is troubled, that is exactly when you need to call on HIM. Call on HIM in time of trouble, as well as in time of blessing.

Now let us examine the words contained in the opening sentence of this lesson: sin, iniquity, transgression. All of these words appear in Psalms 103:10-12,

*"He hath not dealt with us after our **sins**; nor rewarded us according to our **iniquities**. 11 For as the heaven is high above the earth, so great is his mercy toward them that **fear him**. 12 As far as the east is from the west, so far hath he removed our **transgressions** from us."*

Sin is of the physical body. It may be an unlawful act. According to the Scriptures, to disobey the laws of the land is sin. Sin may be as simple as speeding down the road, or taking a pencil from work bought with company money. It is any offence committed against the flesh: sex out of wedlock; fornication; sex with someone other than your spouse, adultery; being a busybody or interfering in matters that don't pertain to you. Sin is something that all human beings commit, whether consciously or by co-mission (sin unknowingly committed). It is because of the sin born in us that we must be mindful, on a daily basis, to pray forgiveness for our sins. That is in part what Paul was saying in, *"I die daily."* He recognized that sin is a part of who we are. We must be vigilant and steadfast to give God all the praise and honor, and to ask for coverage of our sins daily. There are some Christians, who believe stedfastly they are without sin. They are a liar and the truth is not in them. The Scriptures say, "All have sinned and come short of the glory of God." (Rom. 3:23) And, furthermore, the Scriptures say, "He that is without sin among you, let him cast a stone at her" (St. Jn. 8:7) And the Scriptures further say, "If we say that we have no sin, we deceive ourselves, and the truth is not in us." (1 Jn. 1:8) Why? Because he or she lied, which is a sin. Most importantly, the lie is probably the forth worse sin there is. Think about it, breaking the first three commandments are the worse sins we can commit. The lie is forth in my opinion because it was the lie that caused Lucifer and one third of the angels to be *"reserved in everlasting chains under darkness"* (Jude 6) And the lie is what caused the fall of man, Satan said to Eve, *"Ye shall not surely die:"* (Gen. 3:4) when God told Adam *"Ye shall not eat of it, neither shall ye touch it, lest ye die."* (Gen.3:3)

Iniquity has a more deep-seated meaning. Is it sin? Yes, it is absolutely sin. However, iniquity has a co-partner component involving the mind, in addition to that of the physical body.

Iniquity is where evil comes into play. It involves morals, mischief, corruption, wickedness, out right wrong, and intentional harm to others. It represents cruel and unusual behaviors such as, child or elderly abuse; torture; doing what ever it takes for gain of wealth; animal abuse; oppression, racial hatred, and much more. Iniquity is depravity of the mind that leads one to commit physical acts that are destructive to others, and concurrently to themselves. Even more so, iniquity can cause one immediate death and a life long trip to hell. Iniquity is having ones conscious seared. It is a terrible state of soul degradation.

Iniquity may be the cause of mental illness, or perhaps; mental illness may cause people to commit iniquity. Either way, they go hand in hand. Many people, who commit heinous crimes have underlying mental disorder. The only way to fix iniquity is to give the problem over to God. HE can make it all right. Make HIM number One in your life, pray earnestly for forgiveness and help. HE will reach down and help anyone who is trying to help himself, or herself. Lift up your arms for HIM and HE will reach down for you.

Transgression is the bigger loser of these three words. All are bad but this one is a direct offence to God. This word means to revolt or to rebel against God. It is to denounce The One and Only True and Living God. It is apostasy (to turn away from God). This is the person, whose soul is lost. However, it does not necessarily represent doom. This person can still come back to God. Returning to God is key, with regard to all of these words, making God first. HE forgives all our sins, iniquities, and transgressions. There are some ingredients involved in healing us from the affliction of iniquity and transgression that will bring us back to God.

God loves us all. HE does not want to punish us; however, like any good father, HE does chastise us to keep us in line. One of the ingredients involved in returning to God appears in verse 13,

*"Like as a father pitieth his children, so the LORD pitieth them that **fear** him."*

You see, the Omnipotent God of heaven requires us to fear HIS wrath. HE is All-powerful and Almighty. Because of HIS Omnipotence, and Omnipresence, fearing HIM will prevent us from moving out too far to the left or to the right. The father, who teaches his children respect, and godly admiration, in combination with punishment (wrath) when the children disobey, usually raises children of whom, become responsible, God fearing adults. It is what having fear of God does for us as well. Fearing HIM will keep us on the straight and narrow path. Will you be perfect? Absolutely not! Will it keep you away from some of the above negative characteristics? Yes, it will. It will protect you 24/7, against all the wiles of the devil.

Fear of the LORD is a wonderful tool for us to use to our advantage and to HIS delight. Psalm 111:10 says,

*"The fear of the LORD is the beginning of **wisdom**: a good understanding have all they that do his commandments: his praise endureth for ever."*

Do you see the entire scenario? In fear of the LORD, there is constraint, restriction, and limitation, as to what one will, will not do. Their conscience is led by the Holy Spirit to prevent them from ungodly behaviors. The good news is, when we do fall down, we get back up again. Need some more good news? We become smarter in having fear of the Omnipotent God of heaven and earth. Brothers and sisters, let me tell you, wisdom is better than any college degree in preparing us for the world. There is no education system in the world that can prepare us and open up our understanding as the gift of God in granting us wisdom. Take full advantage of this tool in the fear of God. Let me be very clear about this statement. I am in no way implying that college is unnecessary. I am a strong advocate of everyone having the opportunity to attend and graduate from college. Think about it, the wisdom of God, combined with a college education! How high do you want to go?

Do not allow sin, iniquity, and transgression to ruin your life on earth, and cause you to miss out on your heavenly reward, which is, living forever in heaven with

Anthony J. Vance

God. We only get one travel allowance on earth, use it to your benefit. Live life decently and in order on earth and heaven will be your eternal home. Make God your number One. Amen!

Review Questions:

1. Blessing God leads to benefits for the soul:

a. True
b. False

2. God has dealt harshly with us for our sins:

a. True
b. False

3. God's mercy stretches from earth into heaven for those who:

a. Forget about HIM
b. Stop praying
c. Fear HIM

4. Sin, iniquity, and transgression, are the same behaviors:

a. True
b. False

5. Which action does God have for those, who fear HIM:

a. Rejection
b. Sympathy
c. Pity

THE FIRST CHILDREN

KINGDOM BUILDING

O sun and moon, earth and stars, wind that listeth, water of the seas, and all the elements that are, praise ye the LORD, Amen!

The subject of the lesson we are about to embark upon will be taken from multiple sections of the Holy Bible. It is an eclectic collection of Scriptures defining the role God's creations play in life. While this section of study references Psalm 148, it is not entirely focused on Psalm 148. The reason for selecting this chapter for the title is it contains all of the elements this lesson will bring to the forefront of our attention and our thoughts. In fact, we will start off with Psalm 89:9,

*"Thou **rulest** the raging of the sea: when the waves thereof arise, thou stillest them."*

There is no brain, it does not see, it does not hear, it smells not, but; yet, the waters obey. The water is compliant to the dominion and governing (rulest) of God. This is a profound piece of Scripture. Though water has no senses, it honors God through obedience to HIS will. Now turn to Psalm 76:8,

*"Thou didst cause judgment to be heard from heaven; **the earth feared**, and was still,"*

The earth, composed of rock and sand, dirt and clay, stones of varying sizes, density and color. It has no mouth, it has no soul, but; yet, it obeys. Upon the word of God, it stands still. Isn't that amazing? Put into motion by God and told to continue to rotate until I (God) says, stop, be still. This place we call home, the earth, is obedient to the will of God. The greatest point in this verse is this, the earth fears God. This is one of those statements that causes one say, hum, look at God. Amazingly, in fearing God, we honor HIM, and will remain in good standing with HIM. For in fear, we try consistently to make God first in our lives. Proverbs 1:7 discusses the fear of the LORD being the beginning of knowledge. If the earth can be obedient, surely, we humans can as well.

In Psalm 8:3, we find these words,

*"When I consider thy heavens, the work of thy fingers, the moon and the stars, which thou hast **ordained**;"*

How wondrous are thy works O LORD? Built by Thy hands and placed in the heavens with Your Fingers. This is utterly incredible. There is so much significance in this verse, that it causes those, who understand it, to almost burst open with exuberance and praise, and honor to God.

Look at the words closely. All that was made was made by God; all that exists was set in motion by God. HE placed everything in order to perfection. Get this, not only were these orbiting pieces of dirt created by God, they have jobs to perform as well. The word ordained in the above verse has multiple meanings. One meaning is faithfulness. That means that the planets are loyal to God. Another meaning of ordained is to stand. These planets stand up every day glorifying God. Appoint is another meaning of ordained. They have their appointed positions in time and space, all serving their God appointed duties. The word ordained has many other meanings, the last word we will discuss relating to ordained is perfect. The planets are in perfect alignment. They carry out their duties perfectly. They adhere to the perfect will of God. They are perfectly fashioned by God. They are in perfect obedience to God. Surely, if the planets are obedient to God, man can at least put forth some effort to comply with the perfect will of God.

There are many Scriptures that tell us the elements and the planets are directly under the dominion of God. This is what it says in Job 9:6-7,

*"Which **shaketh** the earth out of her place, and the pillars thereof tremble. 7 Which **commandeth the sun, and it riseth not**; and sealeth up the stars."*

Hallelujah to the Father, HE is All Powerful! HE speaks and even the sun is obedient unto HIM. This verse contains multiple words ending in 'th' The 'th' represents a continuous and ongoing process. In other words, the sun is continuously moved (shaketh) by God, ruled (commandeth) by God, and will never shine again (riseth not) if ordered not to shine by God. The planets fear God more than man has fear of God. They are always obedient to God. Somehow, though they have no living soul, they realize that in fearing God, they are from everlasting to everlasting. I know and realize that some Scriptures say, there will be a new heaven and a new earth. That does not mean the present heaven and earth will be destroyed; however, they will be made new in that all sin will be gone. They, as will all people, who are saved, will be a new creation. Just as Jesus rose up in a new glorified body, we too, who are Christians will rise up in our new glorified body. We shall live forever and ever in the presence of our God, our Savior, Jesus Christ. Praise God! Hallelujah to HIS marvelous name.

Now let us examine the verses of Psalm 148:1-6,

"__PRAISE ye the LORD__. Praise ye the LORD from the heavens: praise him in the heights. 2Praise ye him, all his __angels__: praise ye him, all his __hosts__. 3Praise ye him, __sun and moon__: praise him, all ye stars of light. 4Praise him, ye __heavens of heavens__, and ye __waters__ that be above the heavens. 5Let them praise the name of the LORD: for he __commanded, and they were created__. 6 He hath also __stablished them for ever and ever__: he hath made a decree which __shall not pass__."

You see, the stars, the sun and the moon will never pass away. God said so and God does not change nor lie. HE commands everything, the wind, the rain, the moon, all of HIS creation.

These verses are rich in honor and glory to God. This is phenomenally, monumentally, and awesomely, a testimonial to always making God first in our lives. From the most infinitesimal (very small or minute) form of life to the most gigantic planet in existence, honor is given to God. Surely, if the creation itself, worships God, we human beings, the only living souls created, can worship God, making HIM first in our daily lives.

The entirety of this chapter focuses on praising our Creator. Not only should we humans worship God, the planets and the elements do worship HIM. In the rest of the chapter, we find that everything created pays honor to God: cattle, beasts, and all creeping things; the hills and mountains, heaven itself. Even the trees and all plant life worship God. Hallelujah to Your name Father.

The planets and elements are magnificent works that only a Supreme God can make. No one else or any other power exists that can do such marvelous works. When Jesus gave up the ghost, spectacular events occurred. Turn to St. Matthew 27:50-51,

"Jesus, when he had cried again with a loud voice, yielded up the ghost. 51 And, behold, the veil of the temple was rent in

*twain from the top to the bottom; and the **earth did quake**, and the **rocks rent**;"*

O glory to God! The earth cried for the life of Jesus. Not only did the earth cry, it became angry and shook causing a great earthquake. Even the rocks became angry and in their distress and anguish, burst open in expression of their love for Jesus and the Father. I don't know about you, but I don't want any rocks or the earth praising and worshipping God, while I sit, slumber, party, or just stand idle and silent. The best thing that any of us can do is to wake up every morning giving God HIS just due. Thank HIM in the morning, in the evening, and at midnight. Folks, HE is our All in All. Praise HIM, praise HIM, praise HIM!

Each one of us should have an every day goal of setting some time aside to devote to thanking, praising, and worshipping God. We, human beings are considered the highest form of life on earth. HE gave us dominion over all HIS earthly creations. Surely, if the water and rocks can praise HIM, we, who possess a living soul can do the same.

Give God all the honor, all the glory, and all the praise. Bless HIS holy name. Amen!

Review Questions:

1. In HIS Sovereign power, God rules the seas:

a. True
b. False

2. The earth fears God:

a. True
b. False

3. The word ordained in Psalm 8:3, has all of these meanings, except:

a. Faith
b. Stand
c. Abhor
d. Perfect

4. If God chooses to, HE can command the sun to stand still:

a. True
b. False

5. All of creation should praise God:

a. True
b. False

HEAVEN BOUND

KINGDOM BUILDING

Of trial, travel, and making our way toward heaven? All of creation is of God: the good, the bad, and the evil. I have heard it said that, why should I live a Christian life, when God created the evil? There is no fun in being good. There is an understanding that all people have to eventually come to, the end of life in the flesh. We must make a choice between good and evil. For those who choose evil life does not exist, in a good fashion. They are dead from birth and will never live in goodness on the earth, or in the spirit world upon death of the flesh. Yes, they will have all the pleasure their flesh can handle. However, and coincidently, they will have multiples of hardships to endure because of their lifestyle. Many will be tormented through serving time in jail, mental illness, differing medical problems, and above all else, degradation of the soul. They will participate in a myriad of soul destructing activities caused by a seared conscience. In order for us to come into the realization of life, we must be born again by the Spirit, in the spirit contained in our flesh. Hopefully, this text will open our hearts and our minds as to why our earthly journey has been ordained since before the foundation of the world. Every human being has to make a choice about which side of life he or she is on, the God side or the Satan side. Let us begin with Isaiah 45:7-8,

"I form the light, and create darkness: I make peace, and __*create evil*__*: I the LORD do all these things. 8 Drop down, ye heavens, from above, and let the skies pour down righteousness: let the earth open, and* __*let them bring forth salvation, and let righteousness spring up together; I the LORD have created it."*__

This is a magnificent piece of Scripture. Those who say, why should I be good, God created evil? They are absolutely correct in that God created the evil. However, they fail to see why evil was created. I will not try to second guess God and the reason for HIM creating evil. What I hope to do in this lesson is to bring about an understanding of what transpired and led to humankind having to make this earthly journey and having to choose sides.

The word evil in verse 7 represents adversity, affliction, bad, calamity, displease, trouble, and a host of other negative connotations. All that occurs, all that exists, is of God. HE commands the inanimate, and the elements. Everything is under HIS control, and in place by HIS design. HE is Supreme, HE is Sovereign, HE is from Everlasting to Everlasting.

Verse 8 tells us the reason that everything in existence obeys the Father, and why everything that exists, exist. All of these things are examples unto us, humankind. Think about it. If even the elements, that have no soul obey God, how much more should we, humankind, obey? Look closely at the words, *"… let them bring forth salvation, and let righteousness spring up together …"* The first point in this lesson should be coming together in our minds at this time. It is all about choosing righteousness unto salvation. The trials of our travel and the choices we make will determine our final destination. It is so ordered and directed by God; orchestrated by HIM, for the purpose of proving our worthiness and fitness for HIS Kingdom *("I the LORD have created it.")*

Verse 9 says, *"**Woe** unto him that **striveth** with his Maker! Let the **potsherd** strive with the potsherds of the earth. **Shall the clay say to him that fasioneth it, What makest thou?** or thy work, He hath no hands?"*

This verse breaks down in today's language as, who is it that stands against God? I (God) have made you from the dust of the ground. You dare to stand in opposition to ME? We are the work of HIS hands and must give HIM the praise, the honor, and the glory. We must serve HIM only. The word *"Woe"* represents a lamenting against God. Now combine a lamentation against God with the word *"striveth"*. To strive with God is to be in controversy with God; to debate with the rules of God; to be in extreme rebuke of God; to be contemptuous with God; and, to be a complainer of many causes. It is a foolish position for any one to take. We must thank

71

God for what HE does for us. We must accept the good that occurs in our lives and grow from the tragic events that occur in our lives as well. If things in your life are not going well look into the mirror and examine what you see, and furthermore, examine the order of things in your life. First and far most, make God your number one priority of the day. Thank HIM for what HE has done for you. Recognize this, that even if you are not a Christian, God still blesses you. Let me clarify this statement. Every morning you awaken from sleeping, God has blessed you to see another day, another opportunity to get it right. If you are involved in any behaviors that negatively affect your relationship with God, change those behaviors. Will you be perfect or without sin? Absolutely, no! The good news is, by making HIM first, and in acceptance of Jesus Christ, as Lord and Savior, our sins are covered.

The word *"potsherd"* is defined as a piece of pottery or a piece of earth. In verse 9, humans are referred to as a piece of clay. So in combination of the word potsherd with the sentence describing us as clay, the meaning of these two sentences breaks down to, if you have any contention, let it not be with ME, strive clay against clay, your equal. At closer glance, these sentences are about Christians talking to those, who are not God fearing, who are not Christian, to teach the ways of God to bring them into the fold of God. It is all about building the Kingdom of God.

Let me tell you a short story about a woman, whose life is filled with tragic events that have affected her life for many years. Not only have these tragedies negatively affected her, but her children and her children's children. She stated some years ago that her drug addiction is of God. When I personally heard her words with my own ears, chills went throughout my body. My immediate response was to tell her that God does not tell us to do anything that will hurt our bodies or our souls. Her life has been filled with many infractions of the law, leading to jail time. Her husband has served many years of his life incarcerated for possession and trafficking of illegal substances. Her daughters are in and out of bad relationships; and have born children out of wedlock. Furthermore, there is the possibility that she and at least one of the daughter's are involved in prostitution to feed their drug habit. The point in telling this story is, this woman has caused a curse to come upon herself, and upon her children, and upon her children's children because she does not understand that, while God did create evil, HE does not cause us to do evil. It is an act of free will.

The thing that this woman fails to recognize is that while everything is of God, God does not cause us to make bad choices. HE did not tell her to use drugs. She, just as all of us, has the freedom of will. We can choose the God side or the Satan side. Can her awful situation be rectified? It can! God loves all of HIS children. The way for this woman to fix the tragedies occurring in her life is to come to God. She must make God first; accept Jesus Christ as Lord and Savior; and begin to live a Christian life. She has to choose the God side in order for her life to improve.

Her trial and travel must be redirected in order for her to make her way toward heaven.

Verse 10 says, *"Woe unto him that saith unto his father, What begettest thou? or to the woman, What hast thou brought forth?"*

The premise in this verse is basic but magnificent in its presentation. How can the neonate (newborn) say to the progenitors (forefathers), why have you procreated (sexual intercourse) and brought me into this world? Just as the newborn child cannot challenge his parents, neither should we challenge our Father, Who created us.

Verse 23, *"I have sworn by myself, the word is gone out of my mouth in righteousness, and shall not return, **That unto me every knee shall bow, every tongue shall swear**."*

Simply put, the word of God does not change. It is from everlasting to everlasting. The righteousness of God is what we all have to strive for on our earthly journey. For all who are in Christ Jesus, trials will come our way, some more than others. Why? Satan attacks all of God's children trying to weaken their faith. Satan will offer whatever he can to destroy the Christian. He tried to tempt Jesus (St. Matthew 4:1-7). He will work very hard to tempt the Christian, trying to trick the people of God to cause our faith in God to weaken. Satan might even cause the weak Christian to fall into a state of unbelief. Remember this; Satan goes about in the earth seeking whom he may devour (1 Peter 5:8). We must continue in righteousness making our way toward heaven. Whether on the God side or the Satan side, all have to come before the Throne of Grace. God said so.

Our trials, travel, and making our way toward heaven are predestined events of human life. Why do we have to go through trials in our earthly travel? We came from God and have to make our way back to God. There is an example given to us that lends strong credence as to why the trials of our travel are set in place by the word of God. We will now look at some Scripture that provide significant reason for us to prove our worthiness for God's Kingdom. Turn to 2 Peter 2:4,

*"For if **God spared not** the angels that sinned, but **cast them down to hell**, and delivered them into chains of darkness, to be **reserved unto judgment**;"*

This verse is of magnanimous (huge, large, immense) proportion about the trials of our journey. The angels, who were already in heaven with God the Father, turned their backs on HIM. Lucifer, who believed he could overtake the Kingdom of Heaven, deceived them. What a fatal blow to all of the angels that followed him. Cast down to hell where they are imprisoned to the day of judgment. We all come from heaven and must make our way back to heaven. Our trials in our travel are about our worthiness to live in splendid excellence with our Creator in heaven. Will you pass the test of life (birth) unto life (born again) or suffer the same example of the fallen angels?

Though God is a merciful God, HE is also a commanding God. HE gave HIS only begotten Son for us. Turn to Romans 8:32,

*"He that **spared not** his own Son, but delivered him up for us all, how shall he not with him also freely give us all things?"*

My brothers and sisters, God loves us so much that HE gave us one part of the Trinity as a sacrifice for our salvation. In all that God has given us, in HIS love toward us, HE spared not the angels. HE spared not the life of Jesus Christ. In as much, if we are not trying to live a righteous life, and do not accept the sacrificial Lamb as our personal Savior, how much consideration is HE going to have for human beings that follow HIM not? Follow HIM and live life abundantly on your earthly journey. Do not allow the trials of life to be a stumbling block, preventing you from making your way toward heaven. To God be all of the glory. Amen.

Review Questions:

1. God created all of the following except?

a. Light
b. Darkness
c. Evil
d. None of the above

2. All that God created has the foundation of salvation as its main focus?

a. True
b. False

3. A piece of pottery or earth can be described as a?

a. Potsherd
b. Rock
c. Water

4. To woe or strive with God is to be in opposition to God?

a. True
b. False

5. All people, Christian and none-Christian, will one day bow before God Almighty?

a. True
b. False

ISAIAH
CHAPTER 58

PLENTIOUS BOUNTY
IN SHARING

KINGDOM BUILDING

Oh my soul; the core of human life! How are you today? Are you full of the life that God desires for you? Oh my soul, my soul, the everlasting existence of eternity. Live well on earth my soul and heaven will be the place of never ending pleasure for you.

The fact of the matter is; we, Christians, have a duty and an obligation to take care of others. We are to share what we have with others. There are manifold (many, multiple) blessings for those, who give to others freely from the heart. Look at the beginning of blessings involving giving in Isaiah 58:10-11,

*"And if thou draw out thy **soul to the hungry**, and satisfy the **afflicted soul**; then shall **thy light rise in obscurity**, and **thy darkness be as the noonday**: 11And the **LORD shall guide thee continually**, and satisfy thy soul in drought, and make fat thy bones: and thou shalt be like a **watered garden**, and like a spring of water, whose waters fail not."*

In taking care of others, your soul will be satisfied in all that it needs, whether of food, of shelter, or of clothing. Inasmuch, soundness of mind, good health, strong family relations; and as an extra benefit, respect in the community. These two verses are tremendous in speaking on the great outcomes of giving. Look at the word obscurity. This is a place of death, ignorance, destruction, sorrow, and wickedness. However, in giving to others all of the negative connotations of this word, obscurity, disappear in the light shining and emanating from you. Just think what a marvelous world it would be if everyone helped everyone else. There would be no hunger or thirst, everyone would have clothes to wear, shoes on their feet, and access to medical care. Every need of everyone would be satisfied in this simple but important principle of the Holy Bible.

In giving, our soul springs forth as the sprinkler in the middle of the garden. Spraying its mist upon all of the plants giving them the nutrients they need to grow and produce fruit. As long as they are supplied with water, they produce fruit. Giving is one of the most basic principles of Christianity. Helping others leads to production of new fruit in the body of Christ. It is behavior that opens up the eyes of the receiver, causing the light from you to enter into him or her revealing what true Christianity is. Thereby, increasing the number of believers and strengthening the faith of weak Christians. Living a Christian life on earth leads to life eternal in heaven. Glory to God, hallelujah to HIS name!

Verses 12-13 *"And they that shall be of thee shall build the old waste places: thou shalt raise up the foundations of many generations; and thou shalt be called, **The repairer of the breach, The restorer of paths to dwell in.** 13 If thou turn away thy foot from the sabbath, from doing thy pleasure on my holy day; and call the sabbath a delight, the holy of the LORD, honourable; and shalt honour him, not doing thine own ways, nor finding thine own pleasure, nor speaking thine own words:"*

While these two verses are directly related to or speaking on keeping the Sabbath Day holy, there is another significant and important message in these verses also. In order for us to receive the full blessings God has for us, we must in combination with giving, recognize and honor God the Father. In making God our first priority of the day, in recognition of HIM, in prayer, praise, and worship, is a promise to us. That promise being we shall be exalted by HIM, for exalting HIM. What a tremendous title to have bestowed upon an individual, *"The repairer of the breach, The restorer of paths to dwell in."*

Objectively, this title can be viewed as a person, who goes about building up the community or communities. He or she is a help to any and everyone needing assistance. This is the person, who encourages and educates others, and beyond all else, this person promotes God. Glory, glory, glory, to HIS name!

Oh, my soul, my soul. Do that which is good and right, and decent in the name of the Father while walking this earthly journey. Oh, my soul, my soul, take pleasure in the LORD, and all other pleasures will be added unto thee.

Review Questions:

1. Giving honor to God, and giving of what we have to others will lead to obscurity in your life?

a. True
b. False

2. Those, who give to others is compared to a?

a. Withering plant
b. A dark and gloomy day
c. A watered garden

3. In giving to others, combined with honoring God, your blessings will be continual?

a. True
b. False

4. Honoring God and helping others can restore the breaches of many generations?

a. True
b. False

5. The title, "The repairer of the breach, The restorer of paths to dwell in." is an honorable title from God, HIMSELF?

a. True
b. False

JERIMIAH
CHAPTER 18

THE IMMUTABLE GOD

KINGDOM BUILDING

The question is; can God change HIS mind? What a thought this is concerning, The Everlasting and Immutable (Unchangeable) God of heaven and earth. Does HE ever change that which HE has created or make over that HE has made? In Jeremiah, Chapter 18, we will take a close look at the Word of God, examine it, and then render an opinion as to whether God changes things, while HE absolutely remains unchanged. In the first verse of Jeremiah 18, the word of the LORD has come to Jeremiah, the prophet of God. In verses 2-4, there is the story of the potter and the clay vessel he had made. The vessel was marred (imperfect, damaged, blemished). The potter then took the vessel into his hands and fashioned it into a vessel that was appealing or attractive to behold.

Here is the point of the first four verses of Jeremiah 18. These verses are a paradox relating to the continuing message or word from God to Jeremiah in verse 6, to be recorded in the Holy Bible for all peoples, for all generations, and it reads thus:

"O house of Israel, cannot I do with you as this potter? saith the LORD. Behold, as the clay is in the potter's hand, so are ye in mine hand, O house of Israel."

In order to understand why God has made this statement to the prophet for the children of Israel, Jeremiah, Chapters 11-17, will need to be reviewed to bring about clarity of the statement. However, in summation of those chapters, the children of Israel, God's chosen people had done so perversely, that is, worshipping false gods, the prophets rendering false prophesy; there was deceit, human sacrifice, pastors lying and changing the Word of God, gainsaying for wealth, and much more. There was so much ungodliness that God became unhappy with HIS chosen people. They had rebelled multiples of times over the centuries. HE was fed-up with the disrespect this group of people refused to stop engaging therein. Verses 7-8,

*"At what instant I shall speak concerning a nation, and concerning a kingdom, **to pluck up**, and to **pull down**, and to **destroy** it; 8 If that nation, against whom I have pronounced, turn from their evil, I will **repent** of the evil that I thought to do unto them."*

These people have placed themselves in an awful position. To be very blunt, they have not just upset or angered God, HE is ready to damn them to hell. The words pluck up, pull down, and destroy, represent void, undone, loose oneself, perish, and more. HE is ready to destroy them, one and all. The question is; can God change HIS mind?

Verse 10, *"If it do evil in my sight, that it obey not my voice, then I will **repent of the good**, wherewith I said I would benefit them."*

Can God change HIS mind? Here are a people to whom all good has been promised, *"… a land flowing with milk and honey."* (Exodus 3:17) on the verge of having the wrath of God poured down upon them from The One and Only True and Living God. Oh, what a ruinous position to be in! To have all of the promise of God in doing that which is commanded from HIM, and to then go into a backslidden state by worshipping false gods, facing the wrath of The Almighty God. In turning away from God, all the good HE has promised for our respect of HIM, worship, and praise, will be revoked for transgression. Don't get caught in a trap causing God's goodness toward you to be turned into destruction.

Can God change HIS mind? Absolutely, yes! God is Omniscient, Omnipotent, Omnipresent, and HE is The Omni-Everything. Our Supreme Father can do whatever HE pleases. Though it says in the Scriptures, HE never changes. HE can and does change things as HE sees fit to do so. There are behaviors of men that will cause God to turn blessings into curses. One of the greatest of these behaviors is turning away from serving HIM only.

There was a famous husband and wife minister couple, that appeared weekly on television in their own TV ministry. They had a large following of parishioners; furthermore, because they were doing the work God had commissioned them to do, preaching and teaching for Kingdom building, God blessed them to accrue much wealth. In addition, they had built a great empire for Kingdom building. They had it all; unfortunately and sadly, a very human behavior surfaced and what had been the good in them was overtaken by evil. They lost focus and succumbed to greed. In addition, they became involved in immoral and lewd behaviors, which became known to the public, making a mockery of God, and crucifying Christ all over again. To make a long story short, they lost everything.

The husband was convicted of crimes related to fraud or misappropriation of church funds, and other criminal activities also. The husband was convicted of misappropriation of church funds, and sentenced to Federal prison for his criminal activity. Reportedly, while in prison, he was been beaten and raped. How great a punishment the wrath of God can bring forth?

The wife became involved in the pornography industry. Subsequently, she developed cancer and died a slow, tormented and agonizing death. Her appearance for months before the death of her earthly body was that of someone already dead. Her face was very aged with deep set wrinkling. She had the appearance of someone in the final stage of death by starvation.

This awful tragedy occurred for one simple reason, this couple, they forgot about God and began to serve the world. As a result, God changed HIS mind and turned their blessings into curses. What we must do is to always make God our number one priority of the day. Serve HIM only, treat others with respect, and share what we have with others. We must never make a mockery of God or crucify Christ the second time. We all fall short of the glory of God; however, though we all have shortcomings, we must act with discretion, honor and valor. Becoming a public spectacle while preaching to others will cause great plight of affliction, destruction will surely be our reward.

All the days of my life, I have heard the saying, "Prayer changes things." Well, folks, if this statement holds any credence, doing the opposite, not praying and transgression leads to what? Thought, if you believe that prayer changes things, is it not reasonable to believe that the change HE brought about is a change in plan, specifically for your life? Your faith and obedience to the Word of God, though it may be Divine providence, caused a change in direction. HE has to approve the change, if not it remains the same. In example, have you ever prayed for a bad situation to change with no results that you can see, or prayed for a bad situation to improve and receive the desire of your request? The Holy Bible tells us transgression leads to death of the natural body and death of the soul. By the way, prayer only changes things if it is in the Will of God. Surely, The Supreme God of all creation, with all power can do whatever HE pleases. Whatever change HE desires will be HIS decision only. A change we do not want from our Father is for our blessings to become curses. Who determines this outcome? We do, by our choices: righteousness or unrighteousness.

The Israelites refused to give up serving other gods. In HIS anger, God began to mete out punishment to bring them back into line with what HE had commanded them to do. Starting at Jeremiah 18:15, we find words such as: forgotten me; vanity; their land desolate and perpetual hissing; astonished and wag his head; and even more significantly,

*"I will shew them **the back**, and not **the face**, in the day of their calamity."*

Can God change HIS mind? The Scripture is clear in that God never changes. HE remains the same from Everlasting to Everlasting. However, as The Sovereign God of all eternity, and with all might, and with all knowledge, HE can do whatever HE pleases. If we turn our backs on HIM, HE will turn HIS back to us. We, just as the minister couple, who made a mockery of God, will become a disgrace, a hissing, and an astonishment, if we turn our backs to God. Think about this, does God want to punish or bless HIS children? HE loves us and desires the best for us, always.

In transgression, the bountiful blessings HE has for us will be taken away by HIM. Can God change HIS mind? Continuing on with the minister couple and of ourselves, if we transgress from God, our blessings will be revoked, and all, who possess the knowledge of our falling will wag their heads at us. Furthermore, we might die a tormented and humiliating death, without honor. Can God change HIS mind? I don't know about you, but I personally, am not willing to risk it. Though I am imperfect, I give my God HIS just due everyday. I give HIM the honor, the glory, and all of the praise everyday. I fear HIM because HE is to be feared. In fear of HIM, is obedience, and no defiance. Let me be clear in this point. Though we are obedient to the Word of God, we still lack perfection. For you see, we are born in sin and shapen in iniquity. Therefore, all the days of our lives, we will sin. What we must do is to never transgress from God, and never allow our sins to be displayed in an open environment before the public, for all to see. Don't become a public spectacle in your sin. Let me tell you a story about a woman, who stood up in church one Sunday morning. She told the people she wanted to give a testimony. She started telling her story and the people were listening as she spoke. Her story was this, "I am pregnant." The church fell silent as they listened to the first words out of the woman's mouth. She proceeded, "But it's not by my husband." At that point, there were little whispers coming from different areas of the sanctuary. Barely audible you could here the judgment of some: shameful, tramp, Jezebel. At the end of the woman's story, there was complete silence in the sanctuary. However, the woman was not well received by the members of the church, rather, she ended up being ostracized, judged, and criticized, instead.

The point being, live righteously, not piously, pointing the finger at others. We all have sin in us. As long as you live in flesh, sin is present with you. That woman was shunned because of the confession she made. Don't confuse testimony with confession. We all must confess our sins; however, don't confess in an open forum making a spectacle of yourself before men, who will judge you. Go into your closet and confess your sins before God. HE is true to forgive you of all your sins. The worst sin is in turning one's back on God, leading to blessings becoming curses.

Let us examine another verse that exemplifies how a blessing can be lost, and replaced by a curse. We all know that children are a gift from God. Turn to Jeremiah 18:21,

*"Therefore **deliver up their children** to the **famine**, and pour out their **blood** by the force of the **sword**; and let their wives be **bereaved** of their children, and be widows; and let their men be put to death; let their young **men be slain** by the sword in **battle**."*

Did you hear the words of God by the prophet Jeremiah? What a curse this is: woe, horrific, down right utterly tragic: the starvation of the children; death of the children and young men; defeat in battle; a weakened nation because of the loss of men, leaving the women to fend for themselves. As awful as this curse is, it is not all of the punishment to come. The fact is, to bring the wrath of God upon one's self or a group is destruction that can never be matched by any other force. Now turn to Jeremiah 19:5,

"They have built also the high places of Baal, to **burn their sons** *with fire for burnt* **offerings unto Baal***, which I commanded not, nor spake it,* **neither came it into my mind***:"*

This is monumentally significant. The people have violated the commandment of God by building an altar for a false god. Not only did they break the commandment of God, they offended HIM as well, by burning their own children in the fire as sacrifices to this false god named Baal. But, here is the real kicker in this verse, God said, what they have done was never a thought to HIM. Do you get it? Though God is Omniscient, this thought HE says, *"neither came it into my mind:"* Amazing, though God knows everything, this kind of thinking, human sacrifice, HE never allowed just the premise or infinitesimal (minuscule) thought of such an act to come into HIS Sovereign Eternality. I know there is a hum in someone's mind in this verse because of the sacrifice of Jesus. There is no comparison to what these people did. By God, our God, Jesus the Lord, was sacrificed as the Savior of the world. The Israelites were taking human lives in sacrifice to no god at all. It was for their on pleasures.

Anthony J. Vance

They were abusing a part of God's wonderful creation in false worship to something made of wood, or metal, or stone, with no hope of salvation for anyone. But rather, the death of their own body and soul.

At this juncture, we must examine the Word of God from Exodus, Chapter 20, The Ten Commandments. First and foremost, consider the order of HIS commandments. The first commandment, in verse 3 says, *"Thou shalt have no other gods before me."* The first three commandments deal with God being the only God we are to seek. Our God is a jealous God. HIS commandments define what HE will not tolerate from us.

The fourth commandment in verse 20:11, talks about the Sabbath Day and keeping it holy. Here is the point. We are now under grace by the sacrificial blood of Jesus Christ. The blood of Jesus brought us to a new era in religious doctrine. Under the Ten Commandments, working on the Sabbath is prohibited. Now turn to St. Luke 6:3-6,

*"And Jesus answering them said, Have ye not read so much as this, what David did, when himself was an hungered, and they which were with him; 4 How he went into the house of God, and did take and eat the shewbread, and gave also to them that were with him; which it is not lawful to eat but for the priests alone? 5 And he said unto them, **That the Son of man is Lord also of the sabbath**. 6 And it came to pass also on **another sabbath**, that he entered into*

the synagogue and taught: and there was a man whose right hand was withered."

These verses are the forerunners to change in the way we operate today. Jesus declared to the Pharisees, that He, the Son of The Living God, is ruler of the Sabbath and can change the rules as He sees fit to do so. In verses 7-9, is the story of the man with the withered hand. Jesus knowing the thoughts of the scribes and Pharisees asked the question, *"9...Is it lawful on the sabbath days to do good, or to do evil? to save life, or to destroy it?"*

In verse 10, Jesus healed the man's hand and the scribes and the Pharisees were wrought (angry) with Jesus for working on the Sabbath Day. Verse 11 reveals what their thoughts and intent is concerning our Lord Jesus Christ,

"And they were filled with madness, and communed one with another what they might do to Jesus."

From cover to cover, there are no contradictions in the Holy Bible. Though the Old Testament prohibited working on the Sabbath Day, and Jesus authorizes doing what we need to do on the Sabbath Day, it is not contradictory. Here is why, Jesus is God, and God is Jesus. HE can change, though under Divine providence, whatever HE pleases. HE is God! After the coming of our Lord Jesus Christ, working on the Sabbath Day is no longer prohibited. This is a change as phenomenal as the change from the Old Testament to the New Testament.

Beyond that, the part of the Scripture that says for us to keep the Sabbath Day Holy is unchanged. We can work on the Sabbath Day and still keep it holy. Amen.

Back to the above verse in Jeremiah 19:5, let me make this point perfectly clear, human sacrifice is an act brought into play by human beings. God loves all of HIS creation, especially people. HE created us in HIS image, in HIS likeness, and made us a living soul. Therefore, sacrificing people is something that HE never allowed even as a thought. Don't get this concept misconstrued with the crucifixion of our Lord and Saviour Jesus Christ. Jesus' sacrifice is a completely separate entity, not to be co-mingled with any other sacrifice.

Can God change HIS mind? Turn to Genesis, Chapters 18 and 19. Abraham, though he feared God, engaged in conversation with God, about what God purposed to do to the people of Sodom. Six times Abraham spoke to God about not destroying the city, the righteous with the wicked. Six times God said, ok, I will not destroy the righteous with the wicked. Unfortunately, there were less than ten righteous found in the city and it was destroyed. The point being, Abraham, the man of God, convinced God, six times, not to destroy the city for the sake of fifty, down to the sake of ten. Why is this significant? The number 6, represents imperfection, destitute, without God, without Christ. Now get this. God will only allow a certain amount of change. The God of all eternity uses numbers to represent different conclusions. Seven is the number used to represent completion. Six times HE said, ok to Abraham, then it was over. The city was destroyed for lack of righteousness. Can God change HIS mind? Absolutely, yes!

Sodom was very corrupt to the level that God said, I will destroy this people, whom I have created because they regard ME not, they are destitute from ME. Furthermore, the 6 in this verse means in my opinion, this is the last chance they have before I (God) destroys them. Come no more before ME Abraham, to plead for them.

As a basis of support to the above opinion, turn to Genesis, Chapter 2:1-2,

*"THUS the heavens and the earth were finished, and all the host of them. 2 And on the **seventh day God ended his work** which he had made; and he **rested on the seventh day** from all his work which he had made."*

Seven is the number God used to say, it is finished and no further work is needed. Six is the end of a specific intervention.

Let us look at another example of how God can change HIS mind. Turn to Ezekiel, Chapter 20. Again, we find the children of Israel being very recalcitrant (stubborn) in disobedient idol worship. Starting at verse 15, the chapter is telling us about the children of Israel not inheriting the promised land because of whoring (idol worship).

Reading on from verse 15 to verse 24, we find that God removed HIS hand from the children of Israel, HE promises to scatter them among many nations; and that HIS fury is invoked to their demise. Here is the kicker, verses 25-26 read,

*"Wherefore I gave them also **statutes that were not good**, and judgments whereby they **should not live**; 26 And I **polluted them** in their **own gifts**, in that they caused to **pass through the fire** all that openeth the womb, that I might make them desolate, to the end that they might know that **I am the LORD**."*

This verse is extraordinarily profound in its meaning. Statutes that will cause them to fail, certain death, destruction all around them, despair and poverty. Transgression from God will cause your life on earth to become a living nightmare! Why? To hopefully open your eyes for you to see the wrong committed and return to The One and Only True and Living God.

Can God change HIS mind? In this story we have seen a complete reversal of what God's plan was for the children of Israel, they were on their way to a land of plenty. However, because they turned away from God, HE turned the blessings HE had planned for them into curses. You see, it is an awful thing to fall into the hands of The LIVING God. Folks, God does not change. HE is Immutable!

Nonetheless, HE can change HIS mind. This is demonstrated repeatedly in the Holy Scriptures. Let us not confuse HIM not changing- what ever that represents (not to second guess God), with HIM not being able to change HIS mind. Realizing some will say, this is all a part of the plan of God, Divine providence, let me say this; God never intended for anyone to turn their back on HIM. HE always desires the praise and admiration of HIS people. Remember, God is a Jealous God. HE does not tolerate anyone or anything coming before HIM. Furthermore, HE gave us free will to make the choices of how we will live, righteously or unrighteously.

Let us consider one obvious change that God brought about since creating man. Though, in the plan from before the foundation of the world, The New Testament or Covenant of God represents the most striking change in all of existence. This change is a change that will never change again. This change in essence says, I (God) will not tolerate the blood of bulls, rams, goats, or any form of worship than the worship of ME, in the name of MY Son, Jesus Christ. Any other form of worship is idolatry, and punishable by cursing and death.

Can God change HIS mind? The point is this; not only can God change HIS mind; there are thoughts that God never allowed to exist in HIS Omniscient Eternality.

Finally, in this lesson turn to the Book of Job. There we will examine several verses that apply to this lesson.

Job 1:1 reads, *"THERE was a man in the land of Uz, whose name was Job; and that man was **perfect and upright**, and one that **feared God**, and **eschewed evil**."*

Job 2:9, *"Then said his **wife** unto him, Dost thou still retain thine integrity? **curse God**, and die."*

Job 42:10, *"And the **LORD turned the captivity** of Job, when he **prayed** for his friends: also the LORD gave Job **twice as much** as he had before."*

Job was a man of dignity with great moral fiber. He lived as righteously as humanly possible. Above that, Job feared the LORD and had great reverence for the Almighty. As a result, God blessed Job abundantly. As the story goes, Satan had a conversation with God and ultimately God removed the hedge of protection HE had placed around Job. Satan began his assault on Job and great tragedy for Job followed. Everything Job had was lost, including his children. The wife told Job to *"curse God, and die."* Can you imagine the look he must have given her, and I would imagine a tongue lashing like she had never witnessed before.

Satan had hoped that in attacking Job, Job would turn away from The Living God. Howbeit, Job stedfastly remained faithful to God. In the end, Job was blessed more abundantly than prior to Satan attacking him. Job never gave up on God and therewith entering into a state of transgression.

Hopefully, Job's story has brought the point of this lesson to the light. Job remained faithful to the LORD through all of the travail he suffered at the hands of Satan. In the end, God gave Job more than he ever had before. If Job had not remained faithful, all of the torment he suffered at the hands of Satan, would be nothing compared to what would have come from the Almighty. Ultimately, what we do determines how God responds to us, faith in righteousness, or death and destruction in unrighteousness. My Christian friends, don't allow your blessings to become curses. Stay with God and HE will stay with you. No matter what you may be facing, keep the faith. Be like Job, not like the minister couple.

God's course is to have all of humankind with HIM in heaven. HE never changes and HIS plan has always been and always will be to have us, human beings, just as the angels, and all of the hosts of heaven, praise HIM, praise HIM, praise HIM.

So, to answer the questions at the beginning of this lesson, Does HE ever change that which HE has created or make over that HE has made? Absolutely, no! What HE does change is dependent on us. We must continue in the faith, acknowledge that HE is the Sovereign God, every day, and accept Jesus Christ as Lord and Savior. What we must not do is to enter into a state of transgression, or apostatize (stop believing) from God. To fall into a state of disbelief will cause changes from God to come upon us that turns our blessings into curses. God never changes; however,

HE will change what HE has planned to bless us with to cursing for our transgressing from HIM.

Don't allow your blessings to be turned into curses. Give God HIS just due everyday. HE is The Only True, Wise, and Living God. Don't turn your back on HIM, and HE want turn HIS back on you. Halleluiah, Amen!

Review Questions:

1. The paradox in Jeremiah 18:6, uses the example of which of the following?

a. Brick layer
b. Carpenter
c. Potter

2. In Jeremiah 18:7-8, the people are told to repent of their evil and that in doing so, they will avoid which of the following curses?

a. To pluck up
b. To pull down
c. To destroy
d. All of the above

3. The representation in verse 18:10 says, for obedience there are blessings and for transgression, curses?

a. True
b. False

4. In Jeremiah 18:15, the Scripture says, that if we turn our back to God, HE will turn HIS back to us?

a. True
b. False

5. Deliver up their children, famine, death by sword, bereavement, loss of the men in battle, are some examples of how God's wrath can come upon those, who transgress from HIM?

a. True
b. False

6. What is the name of the false god the children of Israel sacrificed their children to?

a. James
b. Michael
c. Jeremiah
d. Baal

EZEKIEL
CHAPTER 26

A CITY LOST, TYRUS
OR ATLANTIS

KINGDOM BUILDING

A city *"never to be found again,"* In the study of mythology, Atlantis is a country that sank into the sea and has not been located since it collapsed, broke apart, and sank into the sea. There have been speculations, as to the location of the mysterious place called Atlantis. In this lesson, we will examine some Scripture that might enlighten us about the mysterious place that may not be a myth in the least.

In the Old World, there was a country in the *"midst of the sea"* called Tyrus. The people of that land profaned against the sanctuary of the LORD God Almighty, against the house of Judah, and against the people of Israel (See Ezekiel 25:3). The Ammonites, distant cousins of the Israelites, inhabited this place called Tyrus. The Great God of heaven and earth became angry with those people because of the disrespect they displayed toward HIM and HIS people.

Ezekiel 26:2 says:

*"Son of man, because that Tyrus hath said against Jerusalem, Aha, she is broken that was the gates of the people: she is turned unto me: **I shall be replenished, now she is laid waste:**"*

The people of Tyrus treated the Israelites like less than human beings, trodden them under foot, as dirt (See Ezekiel 25:6). The people of Tyrus celebrated the terrible treatment of the Israelis' by clapping and rejoicing in the punishment of Israel in sincere exuberance from their hearts. What they did not realize was; God is on their side, The Protector.

Vengeance belongs to the LORD, and HIS judgment is true to the just and unjust alike. In this case, the just are suffering great affliction at the hands of the unjust. *"Aha"* is grief or surprise. To the surprise of Tyrus she will be devastated in total ruin. Both sets of people will see the power of God. Look at Ezekiel 26:14:

*"And I will make thee like the **top of a rock**: thou shalt be a place to **spread nets upon**: thou shalt be **built no more**; for I the LORD have spoken it, saith the Lord GOD."*

This verse tells us that Tyrus is to be destroyed, never to be built again. Moreover, this verse gives us a glimpse of what is to come of this place. Though I am no angler, I believe that the top of a rock is where the fishers spread their nets to dry after they are done fishing, and a good place to fold the nets for their next use. Their nets are cast out and spread forth to capture as many fish at one time as possible. The *"top of a rock"* is barren and desolate, making it the best place to put the nets to prevent them from becoming damaged.

In Ezekiel 25:10, the Word of God says, *"... that the Ammonites may **not** be remembered among the nations."* This verse alone tells us that this place is to disappear forever from the face of the earth.

Ezekiel 26:15: *"Thus saith the Lord GOD to Tyrus; **Shall not the isles shake at the sound of thy fall**, when the wounded cry, when the slaughter is made in the midst of thee?"*

Apparently, from this verse, Tyrus was one island among many islands in that region. The destruction of Tyrus will be very great, and all of the surrounding lands will quake and the noise will be very loud, and heard from miles away. Every country or land around will feel her (Tyrus) destruction, as she falls from glory. In verse 16, because the cry of Tyrus is so great and terrible, that the princes of the surrounding nations will disrobe and sit upon the ground in utter astonishment of Tyrus' demise. They shall tremble in fear for their own fate.

Ezekiel 26:17: *"And they shall take up a lamentation for thee, and say to thee, How art thou destroyed, that wast* inhabited *of seafaring men,* __*the renowned city*__*, which wast* __*strong in the sea*__*, she and her inhabitants, which cause* __*their terror*__ *to be on all that* __*haunt it*__*!"*

Tyrus was a city of great respect and very strong among nations. Other countries feared her because of her power and influence; she controlled the entire region by her might. The word *"haunt"* means to ambush, cause to, seat, and many other words. It is from the prime root word *"yashab."* Tyrus was a bully to say the least and the seat of controlling power of the region.

Ezekiel 26:18: *"Now shall the* __*isles tremble*__ *in the day of thy fall; yea, the isles that are* __*in the sea*__ *shall be* __*troubled at thy departure*__*."*

The destruction of Tyrus will cause great waves in the sea as she falls from glory. I surmise that, great tidal waves and tsunami activity are the cause of the other nations or *"isles tremble."* Their eyes will witness Tyrus sink into the sea. It has to be in their minds also, will our land also sink into the sea?

Ezekiel 26:19: *"For thus saith the Lord GOD; When I shall make thee a desolate city, like the cities that are not inhabited; when I shall bring up the deep upon thee, and* __*great waters shall cover thee*__*;"*

This verse says without a doubt that, Tyrus is heading for ruinous destruction and will disappear into tremendous depths of water. It will sink to the bottom of the ocean, never to be recovered in all of human time.

Ezekiel 26:20: *"When I shall bring thee down with them that **descend into the pit**, with the people of **old time**, and shall set thee in the **low parts of the earth**, in places desolate of old, with them that go down to the pit, that thou be not inhabited; and I shall set glory in the land of the living;"*

This verse draws a parallel between the destruction of Tyrus and the people living on earth prior to the coming of our Lord and Savior Jesus Christ to earth. Those souls were kept in a holding area or prison under the earth.

1 Peter 3:19-20 reads:

"By which also he went and preached unto the spirits in prison; 20 Which sometime were disobedient, when once the longsuffering of God waited in the days of Noah, while the ark was a preparing, wherein few, that is, eight souls were saved by water."

The people of old, upon death of the flesh, had to be kept somewhere until they were preached to about the gospel of Jesus Christ. The ones, who believed His report, when He preached to them in the prison, followed Him out of the prison. The ones, who did not believe on Him, remained in the *"low parts of the earth,"* The people of *"old time"* and Tyrus are gone forever from the face of the earth, all destroyed under water, never to be found again.

Mind you, that is not to say they, the people of old, will not face the day of judgment. Every soul that ever lived and died in unbelief will go before the throne of God for sentencing. The saved have been accounted for by our Lord and Savior, Jesus Christ. Amen.

Ezekiel 26:21: *"I will make thee a terror, and thou shalt be no more: though thou be **sought for**, yet shalt thou **never be found again**, saith the Lord GOD."*

This verse says it all; men will look for you, O Tyrus, but will not find you, you are destroyed forevermore. A city lost, Tyrus or Atlantis? No one knows where Tyrus was located and never will. However, though this is completely a speculation, looking at the world map, Tyrus might have been located in the Pacific Islands. To try to pinpoint exactly where would be ludicrous and for nought because the Bible does not lie. This place, Tyrus will never be found again. It could have been near to Samoa, Japan, Hawaii, or anywhere in that Pacific Island region.

Live a God filled life on earth, eschewing evil, believe on Jesus Christ, and follow the direction of the Holy Spirit. Praise be to God! Hallelujah. Amen.

Review Questions:

1. What word did Tyrus use to ridicule the Israelites:

a. Aha
b. Again
c. Ashamed

2. The LORD God said all of the following to Tyrus except:

a. Top of a rock
b. Be blessed
c. Spread nets upon
d. Built no more

3. The isles near Tyrus shall do what:

a. Fall
b. Shake
c. Sound off

4. All of the following words are used against Tyrus except:

a. Renowned city
b. Strong in the sea
c. Inheritance
d. Haunt it

5. In the destruction of Tyrus the words tremble, troubled, and departure describe Tyrus' impending doom:

a. True
b. False

6. What natural element will cover Tyrus:

a. Mud
b. Sand
c. Water

7. Where will Tyrus' final resting place be:

a. Low parts of the earth
b. Heaven
c. On the mountain tops

8. Tyrus will be discovered and rise to power again:

a. True
b. False

DANIEL
CHAPTERS 1-5

NOT JUST A FIERY FURNACE

KINGDOM BUILDING

We have all heard, most likely, multiples of times, the story of Shadrach, Meshach, and Abednego, in the fiery furnace. In studying the Scriptures surrounding all that was happening to these men, the fiery furnace is only a small portion of what this story teaches us about our Lord and Savior, Jesus Christ, and of our Father, The One and Only True and Living God.

In the First Chapter of Daniel, we find that king Nebuchadnezzar of Babylon, had overtaken Jerusalem, which was under the reign of Jehoiakim, king of Judah. The Babylonians believed in science, magical powers, astrology, sorcery, and the visions of the Chaldeans. King Nebuchadnezzar had erected a large false god and ordered all of the people under his reign to worship that false god. In the first part of our study, turn to Daniel 1:7, and there we will find one of the first acts committed by Nebuchadnezzar after he had taken Judah captive.

"Unto whom the prince of the eunuchs gave names: for he gave unto Daniel the name of Belteshazzar, and to Hananiah, of Shadrach; and to Mishael, of Meshach; and to Azariah, of Abednego."

The first question is; what is in a name? There are several points to be made in this multi-faceted lesson of these men of faith. From the outset, changing their names in effect is an attempt to reduce these men to a lesser status by trying to remove their birth names. To remove one's given name is akin to disenfranchising that person from their heritage. It is also a method used to make a person more compliant to the authority of their ruler. When you take away one's identity that person becomes a weaker vessel. In fact, if you take away the given name of a nation of people, they become no people and just a part of the culture they are consumed into.

Next in this lesson, we find that Daniel, though taken into captivity along with Shadrach, Meshach, and Abednego, was treated differently because he interpreted the dream of Nebuchadnezzar. Look at verses 2:46-47,

*"Then the king Nebuchadnezzar fell upon his face, and worshipped Daniel, and commanded that they should offer and oblation and sweet odours unto him. The king answered unto Daniel, and said, Of a truth it is, **that your God is a God of gods**, and a Lord of kings, and a revealer of secrets, seeing thou couldest reveal this secret."*

There are several points in these verses to discuss. First, the king recognized that Daniel was acting by the influence of The True God of heaven and earth. Next, because Nebuchadnezzar recognized the power Daniel was acting under, he did no harm to Daniel, and in fact made Daniel a great man in his kingdom.

The king made a decree in Daniel 3:11, with regard to the false god he had made.

"And whoso falleth not down and worshippeth, that he should be cast into the midst of a burning fiery furnace."

Here is the irony of verse 3:11, although Nebuchadnezzar believed the God of Daniel to be The True God, he also continued to worship the false God he had made. Another observation in our lesson thus far is, was Daniel required by the king to worship this false God or was he exempted because he served The Living God?

As the story goes, Hananiah, Mishael, and Azariah, refused to bow before the god of Nebuchadnezzar and were tossed into the fiery furnace. The furnace was heated seven times its normal temperature. Here is the point, the number 7 represents completion; therefore, for Shadrach, Meshach, and Abednego, it meant your victory is already at hand. You will come out of the furnace and be promoted to a position of authority, better off than before entering the fire. Look at verse 3:27, *"… nor the smell of fire had passed on them."* Great God in heaven! They were breathing fresh air in the middle of all consuming smoke. Furthermore, as we have all heard before, Jesus was also in the fiery furnace with His faithful followers.

To answer the above question, was Daniel required to bow to the false god? No! Proceeding on, there was a phenomenal change on the way for Nebuchadnezzar. For you see, there are no astrologers, magicians, soothsayers, Chaldeans, or sorcerers that can achieve the level of wisdom, vision, direction, or knowledge than a man of God. Everything that happens, happens for a reason and a purpose. Here is the phenomenal change of Nebuchadnezzar, turn to Daniel 4:34,

*"And at the end of the days, I Nebuchadnezzar lifted up mine eyes unto heaven, and mine understanding returned unto me, and I **blessed the most High, and I praised and honoured** him that liveth for ever, whose dominion is an **everlasting dominion**, and his kingdom is from generation to generation:"*

Here is the point, sometimes we have to endure punishment for not complying with the God of all eternity. Let me clarify the "sometimes" in the above sentence, it applies to idol worship, apostasy, and transgression, not that it cannot apply to sin. However, we all sin and come short of the glory of God. Sin and transgression though sometimes used interchangeably are separate behaviors and or thought processes. Let me digress somewhat to make the point clear about the punishment of Nebuchadnezzar. Nebuchadnezzar, because he refused to stop worshiping the false god of his own creation, and continued to invoke all of the people to practice idol worship, had to be brought low or abased. His punishment is described in Daniel 4:33,

*"The same hour was the thing fulfilled upon Nebuchadnezzar: and he was **driven from men**, and did **eat grass as oxen**, and his body was wet with the dew of heaven, till his **hairs were grown like eagle's feathers**, and his **nails like birds' claws**."*

King Nebuchadnezzar fell from his throne and was made to eat grass as an ox. He was un-kept, dirty, and driven away from other people. He in effect became no more than an animal of the field because of idol worship. Can you imagine the humiliation Nebuchadnezzar experienced? He suffered these things to open up his eyes and understanding that God is God and that there is no other God, but God.

Nebuchadnezzar became a convert to The One and Only True and Living God. By being abased Nebuchadnezzar gained full insight about The Living God of heaven and stopped practicing idol worship. Therefore, God restored the kingdom unto him, not just restored, but restored, *"… excellent majesty was added unto me."*

There is more to the Book of Daniel than the fiery furnace. Daniel is about making God first, always. We must never allow anything to come before our Father in heaven. Not making HIM first might result in punishment for the violator. Making HIM first will bring you victory and blessings. Now turn to Daniel 4:37,

*"Now I Nebuchadnezzar **praise** and **extol** and **honour** the King of heaven, all whose works are truth, and his ways judgment: and those that walk in pride he is able to **abase**."*

This verse says it all, give God HIS just due or you will be brought low! Amen!

Review Questions:

1. What was the name appointed to Daniel by Nebuchadnezzar:

a. Belteshazzar
b. Meshach
c. Shadrach
d. Abednego

2. After Daniel revealed the secret to Nebuchadnezzar, Nebuchadnezzar confess' God is God:

a. True
b. False

3. All of the following were tossed into the fiery furnace except:

a. Shadrach
b. Daniel
c. Meshach
d. Abednego

4. When Nebuchadnezzar returned to his understanding, he did which of the following:

a. Blessed the most High
b. Praised and honored God

c. Accepts God's kingdom as everlasting
d. All of the above

5. When Nebuchadnezzar received punishment from God, what did he eat:

a. Grass
b. Meat
c. Vegetables
d. Fish

6. Which of the following describe Nebuchadnezzar's appearance:

a. Hair like eagle's feathers
b. Nails like bird's claws
c. None of the above
d. Both a and b

7. Praise, extol, and honor are words Nebuchadnezzar used to honor God:

a. True
b. False

THE FEROCIOUS
MOUTH TAMED

KINGDOM BUILDING

Over the many years of attending Sunday morning worship service and attending Bible School, we have all heard the story of Daniel in the lions den repeatedly. The story about Daniel in the lions den has more information to discuss than the obvious, Daniel not becoming a meal for the lions. While this significant and important story is included in this lesson, there is much other valuable information in this story that preachers fail to bring out in their sermons.

Yes, there was Daniel in the lions den and he was totally unharmed by the loins. This was phenomenal because the protection of God was upon Daniel. The focus of this lesson is; why was Daniel thrown into the den of lions?

At that time in Babylon, king Belshazzar, was having a party for one thousand guests. They were having a wonderful time and drinking wine, they were all very festive. King Belshazzar was in possession of the gold and silver vessels that were taken from the Temple of God, during the captivity. Belshazzar ordered those vessels to be brought into the party so that the important dignitaries at the party could drink from the precious gold and silver cups. In addition, as they were drinking from the cups that belonged in the House of God, they gave praise to the false gods they had made.

Daniel 5:4 reads: *"They drank wine, and praised the gods of gold, and of silver, of brass, of iron, of wood, and of stone."*

Of course, our God, Who is a Jealous God, became offended by the actions of Belshazzar and the others attending the party. Within the same hour, they began to drink from the vessels that belonged in the House of God, a very significant thing occurred. Examine verse 5:5:

*"In the same hour came forth fingers of a man's hand, and wrote over against the candlestick upon the plaister of the wall of the king's palace: and the **king saw** the part of the hand that wrote."*

The king seeing this hand is very important in two points: one- that this was a spiritual presence with a physical manifestation, and two- only the king saw the hand. This phenomenon was so disturbing to the king that his countenance (affect, mood, demeanor, attitude) changed. In fact, what the king saw caused a physical change in his body structure. Verse 5:6 says:

*"Then the king's **countenance was changed**, and his thoughts troubled him, so that the joints of his loins were loosed, and **his knees smote one against another**."*

In effect, the king is now what some refer to as, knock kneed. The shape of his legs changed from their normal position to that of his knees knocking together as he walked. It gave Belshazzar the appearance of having a physical deformity. Belshazzar was playing with fire, that is, he offended The One and Only True and Living God. Belshazzar called upon the astrologers, the Chaldeans, the soothsayers, and others to interpret the writing the hand had made upon the plaister. None of the them could interpret the writing. The words written upon the plaister are "... *MENE, MENE, TEKEL, UPHARSIN.*"

When the queen learned of the situation, she came before the king and informed him of Daniel, who had been appointed master of the wise men in the king's dominion, under Nebuchadnezzar. Daniel was summoned to the party by king Belshazzar and shown the writing on the wall. The king promised Daniel the best gifts possible if he could interpret the writing. Of course, Daniel being a man of God, refused the gifts. Daniel then read and interpreted the above words. The full interpretation of the above words are found in Daniel 5:26-28. Essentially, what the words mean is this, your kingdom shall be taken away from you and divided among other peoples, and you will be punished for worshipping false gods.

Now turn to Daniel 5:21 and hear the punishment of Nebuchadnezzar, Belshazzar's father:

*"And he was driven from the sons of men; and his heart was made like the beasts, and his dwelling was with the wild asses: they fed him with grass like oxen, and his body was wet with the dew of heaven; **till he knew that the most high God ruled** in the kingdom of men, and that he appointeth over it whomsoever he will."*

There is a tremendous message in this verse, the most powerful man in the kingdom, the king, has been rendered to the level of an animal of the field. He became no more than an ox eating grass and sleeping outside in the open field. Can you imagine the humiliation of the king? His punishment continued until he recognized that God rules everything. Upon giving honor to God, Nebuchadnezzar's kingdom was restored unto him.

Very importantly, Belshazzar knew what had transpired with his father, Nebuchadnezzar for idol worship. Yet, he observed these pagan practices anyway. After Daniel interpreted the words MENE, TEKEL, UPHARSIN, and PERES, the king appointed him third ruler of the kingdom and did dress him in royal apparel. Unfortunately, for Belshazzar, that same night his demise was at hand. This is found in Daniel 5:30.

Darius became king at that time. He really liked Daniel because he knew that Daniel was under the influence of the Spirit of God. Here is where the trouble starts for Daniel. Darius had appointed many presidents over the country and Daniel had favor over them all. Of course, a spirit of jealousy rose up in the other presidents. They then conspired together and came up with a plan to make ruin of Daniel. What these presidents did, realizing that Daniel only practiced true religion, proposed a decree to the king to entrap Daniel in a snare for his demise, a decree for idolatry. This portion of the story is found in Daniel 6:4-9. These presidents knew that Daniel would never allow anything or anyone to come before his God. Therefore, Daniel would continue his daily ritual of praise, worship, and honor to God.

Now examine Daniel 6:10: *"Now when Daniel knew that the writing was signed, he went into his house; and his **windows being open** in his chamber toward Jerusalem, he kneeled upon his knees three times a day, and **prayed, and gave thanks** before his God, **as he did aforetime**."*

Daniel knew that to disobey the decree of the king would mean certain death. Inasmuch, he was not willing to make any person his first focus. That place for Daniel is reserved for The One and Only True and Living God. Though to break the king's decree would bring about swift punishment from the king, Daniel continued to worship God in plain view for all to see. Of course, the other presidents observed Daniel in his practice of worshipping God and reported this infraction to the king. Their plan had worked, they will now be free of Daniel having preference over them.

The king, who really favored Daniel, then realized when the other presidents came to him and reported Daniel, that it was a trap. Unfortunately, a decree from the king must be carried out without question, even for the king himself. Verse 6:14 reads:

*"Then the king, when he heard these words, was **sore displeased with himself**, and set his heart on Daniel to deliver him: and he **laboured** till the going down of the sun to deliver him."*

King Darius was filled with grief for Daniel because he knew that he could not reverse the decree. The king was distraught and delayed delivering Daniel as long as he possibly could without disobeying his own decree. In Daniel 6:15, the men pressed upon the king and reminded him of the law. Verse 6:16 reads:

*"Then the king commanded, and they brought Daniel, and cast him into the den of lions. Now the king spake and said unto Daniel, Thy God whom thou servest continually, **he will deliver thee**."*

This is a fantastic saying from the king because the king is full of the faith that God will protect Daniel. The king's faith is no doubt strong and above reproach in that, God will protect Daniel in the midst of a very dangerous situation. If only we, Christians today, could muster up this same faith, what a different world it would be today.

Daniel 6:18: *"Then the king went to his palace, and **passed the night fasting:** neither were instruments of musick brought before him: **and his sleep went from him.**"*

The king loved Daniel and even more so, he loved God. This terrible situation bothered the king so severely, that he could not sleep that night. He was depressed and refused to allow the musicians to play the customary music of the evening. In honor of God, for the safety of Daniel, the king also refused to eat food, fasting as an act of faith that Daniel shall be unharmed by the lions. The next morning the king went very early to check on Daniel. He went in *"haste"* like a father coming to meet his child, whom had been lost and now is found.

Daniel 6:20: *"And when he came to the den, he cried with a **lamentable voice** unto Daniel: and the king spake and said to Daniel, O Daniel, servant of the living God, is thy God, whom thou servest continually, able to **deliver thee from the lions**?"*

This word *"lamentable"* means to wail and mourn out loud, to be filled with grief, to express sorrow and or regret. The king was on the verge of an emotional breakdown. This speaks volumes about the love the king has for Daniel. The king is the most distinguished dignitary of the entire state. He is to be poised, reserved, controlled, and have command of his faculties at all times. In his state of emotional distress, the king asked Daniel if God had delivered him from the lions. The question is not whether

God could deliver Daniel, but rather, was it God's plan to deliver Daniel from the lions. Daniel answered the king to let him know that all is well, and informed him that, God had sent an angel to protect him from the lions by shutting up the mouth of the lions.

Daniel 6:24: *"And the king commanded, and they brought those men which had accused Daniel, and they cast them into the den of lions, **them, their children, and their wives**; and the lions had the **mastery** of them, and brake all their bones in pieces or ever they came at the **bottom of the den.**"*

Daniel was innocent of doing anything wrong in the kingdom. Those presidents, because of jealousy, conspired to cause harm to a guiltless man. This is a very dangerous situation for the accuser(s). Look at what their fate ended up being; they were thrown into the very trap they conspired to have Daniel executed therein. We must be very careful about planning to cause harm to others, especially, those under the protection of God the Father. Not only does doing wrong to others lead to harm for the false accuser(s), it can cause harm to the entire family unit. Those presidents, their children, and their wives, all became meals for the lions.

Listen! When you act in evil, consider this; your father, mother, brother, sister, child, and even your cousin, aunt, uncle, could bear the brunt of your evil. These verses are a warning against doing evil of any kind. God is the Avenger, keep evil out of your life. Amen.

The word *"mastery"* means, with great skill, superior, and dominion. Those lions, bone by bone, destroyed all of the evildoers. Every bone of every person was broken to pieces. In addition to the lions breaking their bones, some of the bones were also broken when their bodies came into contact with the den floor. Observe this: in verse 16, Daniel was *"cast"* into the lions den, but sustained no injury when he landed on the dens floor. The word cast means to throw or to fling. You see, God already had Daniel's back before Daniel was ever accused or thrown into the den of lions. This is a very significant point to see! As a child of God, who believes on Jesus Christ, and following the direction of the Holy Spirit, you too, have God's protection all about everything you do. Those, who come up against you, will fall into the same trap they have set for you. Glory to God!

Daniel 6:26: *"I make a decree, That in every dominion of my kingdom men **tremble and fear** before the God of Daniel; for he is the living God, and stedfast for ever, and his kingdom that which shall not be destroyed, and his dominion shall be even unto the end."*

The significant aspect of this verse is straight forward and to the point. The fear of God is the instrument that we all must have in order to keep ourselves on the narrow path in life. That fear keeps us humble and prevents us from straying too far away from our heavenly Father.

In closing this lesson, Daniel was thrown into the lions den for several reasons: he had favor of the king over the other presidents; he was under the hand of God, causing all that he did to prosper and the other presidents became jealous of Daniel; and he refused to acknowledge any god other than The True and Living God. My brothers and sisters, don't let anyone take away your joy and blessings, by influencing you in the wrong direction in life. Always give God HIS just due each day of your life. God is priority One. Amen.

Review Questions:

1. The dignitaries at the king's party drank wine and worshipped gods made of all of the following except:

a. Wood
b. Stone
c. Glass
d. Silver, brass, and iron

2. What was the time period that the hand appeared and wrote upon the plaister at the party:

a. Two hours
b. One day
c. One month
d. One hour

3. When the king's countenance changed, a physical change in his body also occurred, which was:

a. He became blind
b. He fainted
c. His knees smote together

4. Nebuchadnezzar, Belshazzar's father for punishment became the equivalent of an animal:

a. True
b. False

5. When the presidents approached the king for a new decree about worship, Daniel complied with the new rules:

a. True
b. False

6. After the king realized what was going on with Daniel, the king said to Daniel which of the following:

a. You should have complied with the decree
b. Thy God whom thou servest continually, he will deliver thee
c. I will punish you for failing to obey my orders

7. The king did all of the following the night Daniel was thrown into the lions den except:

a. Fast
b. Listen to music
c. Slept well
d. Continue to celebrate

8. The next morning, the king went to see about and made a lamentable cry for Daniel:

a. True
b. False

9. The lions made a feast of the presidents, their children, and their wives:

a. True
b. False

10. The new decree from the king ordered the people to:

a. Continue to worship false gods
b. Keep away from Daniel
c. Tremble and fear the God of Daniel

JONAH
CHAPTERS 1-4

PREACHING TO THE LOST

KINGDOM BUILDING

Jonah, the fish, our God, and our Lord and Savior, Jesus Christ; the full account of the story. What a glorious story this is, more than haven being swallowed by a large sea creature and remaining there for three days. The story is phenomenal because there is a parallel to the story that is not told completely during worship events on Sunday morning or in Wednesday night Bible study.

In this story, Jonah was commanded by God to perform a mission in another country. The LORD GOD, told Jonah to go to Nineveh because a great wickedness was going on there; however, Jonah decided to disobey God and fled to Joppa, where he could board a ship going to Tarshish. However, the Omniscient God of heaven and earth rebuked Jonah's plan by sending a great wind upon the ship, a terrible tempestuous storm that nearly tore the ship apart. The shipmaster and the mariners were very afraid, moreover, Jonah, in all that was happening, was below deck asleep. The shipmaster awakened Jonah and told him to get up and pray to God for the safety of the crew and the ship.

Jonah was asked many questions by the shipmaster and had revealed to him and to the crew that, he was fleeing from the presence of the LORD, an impossible task to say the least. Jonah told them to throw him overboard to keep harm away from them. At first, the decision was to keep Jonah on board the ship; however, the tempest would not let up; therefore, the men eventually threw Jonah over board. Jonah 1:17 reads:

*"Now the LORD had prepared a **great fish** to swallow up Jonah. And Jonah was in the belly of the fish **three days and three nights**."*

This great fish swallowed up Jonah and he lived there 3 days and 3 nights, unharmed by the digestive enzymes in the fish's stomach. During his three-day journey in the fish's belly, Jonah was taken to the depths of the ocean, where he saw great mountains under the sea. What a fascinating tour it must have been! Another point to make about the story of Jonah is that, when this story is told, the fish is always referred to as being a whale. The Holy Bible does not call it a whale, but rather, a *"great fish."*

Now look at this, Jonah 1:5 says: *"… But Jonah was gone down into the sides of the ship; and he lay, and was fast **asleep**."*

Do you see any parallels between this story and another very famous and historical story in the Holy Bible? This story is a fascinating and phenomenal occurrence in the history of humankind. Hold on, the tie end to this parallel is coming. This story is fascinating and it is unfortunate that many clergy fail to get this information out to the parishioners. Inasmuch, we all have the responsibility to study the Bible for ourselves (See 2 Timothy 2:15).

Jonah describes his 3 day stay in the belly of that great fish as, "... *the belly of hell...*" This is found in verse 2:2. Jonah felt that his life had reached an all time low, and in fact, it had. However, he came back to his senses and realized there was only one way out of this mess, and that is, to call upon the name of, "... *O LORD my God.*" This is found in verses 2:6-8. After Jonah called upon the name of the LORD, he received his commission from God the second time. Jonah 2:2 reads:

*"Arise, go unto Nineveh, that great city, and **preach** unto it the **preaching that I bid thee**."*

Jonah had been commissioned by God to preach the gospel to the people of Nineveh; even so, he chose to disregard the order he received from God and do his own thing. God was watching, as always. The ship that Jonah boarded was in for a great adventure before it ever left the dock. Jonah is providing us with a great example of what we have to do within this story about receiving commandments from God. Folks, when God tells you by dream, vision, or revelation, to do something, do it. If not your fate is in your own hands. Don't think you can escape the God of heaven and earth, for HE is ALL KNOWING.

Let us continue on with this remarkable Bible story. Jonah 3:4:

*"... Yet **forty days**, and Nineveh shall be overthrown."*

After Jonah received his whipping from God, he went on to Nineveh, as God had commanded him to do and prophesied to the people of Nineveh. Fear came upon the people and they repented of their sins, and put sackcloth upon their bodies and sat in ashes. The king then made a decree to the people telling them what to do to prevent the disaster from happening to them. The king was very sincere about this, to the point that his decree included the animals. This is found in verses 3:7-8.

In order to make clear the *"forty days"* parallel, we will have to examine Saint Luke, Chapter 4, verse 2, and it reads:

*"Being **forty days tempted** of the devil. And in those days he did eat nothing: and when they were ended, he **afterward hungered**."*

The number 40 represents a trial or test period. Even our Lord and Savior, Jesus Christ went through a test period: He was 40 days in the wilderness being tempted of Satan. Oh, but glory be to God, He passed the test with flying colors. Jesus passing the temptation afforded all of us the opportunity to come to God, in the name of Jesus. Now we can all come into HIS Glorious Kingdom, in our belief and calling on the name of JESUS. Realizing some might say, Jesus was under the protection of the Holy Spirit let me make this perfectly clear: the Holy Spirit was not upon Jesus during the trial period. The Spirit came to Jesus after the trial ended; examine Saint Luke 4:14. Another reason we know the Spirit was not preventing Satan from being successful is this, light and dark cannot occupy the same space at the same time, therefore, in order for Christ to have a period or trial of temptation, the Spirit moved out of the way and Satan had free reign to speak with Jesus. In Saint Luke 4:5, it says, *"And the devil, taking him up into an high mountain ..."* Furthermore, look at the above verse again: the main object in this verse to let us know that at that point Christ was a completely human entity is this, when the trial was concluded, Christ was hungry.

Because the people of Nineveh repented of their evil, God decided to pardon them of their crimes against HIM. This is found in Jonah 3:9-10. In Jonah, Chapter 4, we find that Jonah became very angry that the LORD had decided to spare Nineveh. Jonah despaired about the situation to the point that he thought it better to just die. Howbeit, God had a plan to show Jonah why HE did what HE did in sparing Nineveh.

Jonah 4:11 reads: *"And should not I spare Nineveh, that great city, wherein are more than **sixscore thousand persons** that cannot discern between their right hand and their left hand; and also **much cattle**?"*

We serve a merciful God, Who loves us all tremendously. Jonah's mission was to preach to the people to bring them back into line with what God expected and required of them. God did not want to loose that great population of people, nor the animals. In conclusion, the mission or plan of God was to provide the people with a second chance at life. What a wonderful God we serve. God does not want any of us to perish. Jonah's mission was for the saving of souls, just as Christ came to make a way for all of us to have a second chance at life.

Did you catch the parallels of Jonah's journey in comparison to Christ's earthly journey? Christ came to preach the gospel for the saving of souls; Jonah preached to Nineveh for the saving of souls. Christ was 3 days in the prison preaching to the souls in the prison (1 Peter 3:19); Jonah was 3 days in the fish's stomach preparing his sermon to Nineveh. Jesus was asleep in the lower part of the ship when the tempest was upon the ship (Matthew 8:24). Jonah was asleep in the lower part of the ship. Christ was tempted of Satan 40 days in the wilderness; the people of Nineveh had 40 days to decide on repentance or face certain destruction.

Preaching to the lost is what we all must do for our brothers and sisters, who are lost. We must teach, preach, and testify to others to the honor and glory of God. Every one of us should every day of ours lives take some time out of our day to honor God. Personally, I take time every morning to give God HIS just due before leaving my house for work or wherever I'm going. Find the time daily, in your life to make tribute to God and HE will reward you for your honoring HIM. Glory to your name Father! Amen.

Review Questions:

1. The Holy Bible describes the great creature that swallowed up Jonah as:

a. Whale
b. Walrus
c. Fish

2. What was Jonah doing when the tempest was upon the ship:

a. Resting
b. Writing
c. Sleeping

3. Jonah's mission to Nineveh was to preach to the evildoers:

a. True
b. False

4. The people of Nineveh had how many days to repent before destruction would come upon them:

a. 20
b. 30
c. 40
d. 50

5. After the people repented, God spared them and the animals:

a. True
b. False

MALACHI
CHAPTER 3

WHAT DO I GIVE

KINGDOM BUILDING

This lesson has to do with our giving. What does the Holy Bible require us to do to be blessed and to be a blessing to others? The verse in Malachi 3:8, asks the question, *"Will a man rob God?"* Believe this; we all rob God regularly because we are not fully versed on the principles of giving. Many ministers, pastors, and preachers, misuse this verse for the wrong reasons, that is, monetary gain or as the Bible calls it, *"filthy lucre."* These clergy leave out what true giving is all about in order to fill the church coffers with money. Some misuse the Scriptures for personal gain as well, preaching for the money, and not for the saving of souls. In this lesson, we will visit many Scriptures that explain in full detail how we are to give and what to give.

Malachi 3:8 reads: *"Will a man rob God? Yet ye have robbed me. But ye say, Wherein have we robbed thee? In tithes and offerings."*

First point to make about this verse is this; there is a great difference between the tithe and the offering. The tithe is ten percent of whatever you have newly obtained. It is ten percent of the first rewards of your labor. The offering is what is given above the ten percent. The giving of tithes and offerings is not necessarily money. These can be time, service, talent, and so forth. I have often heard ministers say, giving tithes come before taxes are deducted, it is ten percent of your gross earnings. I would like for one minister to show where that is written in the Holy Bible. In fact, the taxes taken out of our check is not ours, it is the governments; therefore, it is simply not correct for ministers to make such a statement. I am personally offended by theoretical nonsense. If you believe the taxes taken out of your check belongs to you, go to the tax office of your city, county, state, or federal agency and request your money. All I can say is, good hope to you in getting it.

The first mention of the word tithes comes in Genesis 14:20 and it reads:

"And blessed be the most high God, which hath delivered thine enemies into thy hand. And he gave him tithes of all."

The most important fact in this verse that we must understand is, at this point, there is no commandment from God to give the ten percent. This was a gift from Abram to Melchizedek, because Melchizedek prayed a blessing upon Abram. However, I do believe this is the forerunner for the commandment to come regarding our giving.

Abram, being a true man of God, was blessed and highly favored by God. You see, Abram was a very wealthy man, turn to Genesis 13:2:

"And Abram was very rich in cattle, in silver, and in gold."

Let me share a personal story with you about giving. One day, I was traveling to Arkansas to visit my children. As I was driving down the road, which I had traveled many times before, I approached an intersection with a stop sign. As I came to a stop, something in my conscience said to me, turn right, turn right, turn right. I had no reason to make a right turn at that intersection; it was out of my way, and it was also a road I had never traveled before. I followed the direction the voice had given to me and made the right turn. At the end of that road was a gas station, I decided to stop at that gas station to get a cup of coffee. As I was about to leave the station, a woman approached my car and knocked on the window. I rolled the window down a little to hear what she was saying to me. She told me that she needed $10 for gas to get back home to Texas. Of course, I immediately thought, what kind of scam is she pulling? Then she said some things to me that was somewhat compelling. As I listened to her story, I became convicted about how God has blessed me, and how wrong it would be not to help the woman if her story is true.

This is what the woman said to me. She had been to Chicago to attend her mother's funeral. A few miles up the road from where we were at the gas station, a tractor-trailer had run her off of the road into the median. Her car was stuck in the median and she had to be pulled out by a tow truck. All the money she had, $25, she paid to the tow truck driver. Continuing on she said to me, with a look on her face and body language of desperation, my car is over there, you can see my driver's license and my car tag, and I have my little girl with me. Please mister, please, $10 is all I need.

After hearing the woman's story, I thought, if she is pulling a scam, let it be on her, but I will do what God would have me to do. I told the woman to pull up to the gas pump and I will put gas in your car. She again stated, just $10 will get me home. I said, Ma'am, Dallas is 350 miles from here, $10 might get you to the Arkansas, Texas border. I filled the woman's car with gas. As I was pumping the gas, she took the little girl from the car.

There was something about the child that caused me to ask the question, Ma'am, have you fed her? She replied, no, I don't have any money, I paid the tow truck driver all the money I had, he wanted $50 but I didn't have it. I finished pumping the gas into the car, and reached into my wallet and gave the woman some money and told her to get the baby something to eat. The woman hugged me for a long while, and wished the blessings of God upon me. As I was leaving, I observed the woman and the child going into the gas station. I then decided to wait in the parking lot to see what the woman was doing, a few moments later they came out of the gas station with some food items. I then drove away from the gas station at that point.

Glory to God, my Christian brothers and sisters! A few weeks later, I went to my mailbox, and, lo, from an unexpected source, I had received a check sufficient to cover the cash I gave to the woman to buy food. One week later, I again went to my mailbox, lo and behold, there was a second check in there. But, get this, the check was 10 times the amount of what it took to fill the woman's gas tank. Glory, glory, glory, to God! You see, you can't beat God's giving. Let me say this before returning to our lesson of Malachi, what if I had not listened to that voice that told me to turn right? What might have occurred with that woman and her child? Even more importantly, what might I have lost for being disobedient?

Abram's gift to Melchizedek was simply that, a gift. When we give from our heart to help others, God, honors that gift and will increase what you have in order for you to continue to bless others. As for tithing, it is meant to spread the fruits of our labor to show love for others and to help guide them into the Christian family. When Abram gave Melchizedek the 10 percent, there was no law or commandment for tithing at that point. The commandment to tithe does not come about until the time of Moses. Turn to Leviticus 27:30:

"And all the tithe of the land, whether of the seed of the land, or of the fruit of the tree, is the LORD'S: it is holy unto the LORD."

In Leviticus, we find multiple laws given to the children of Israel, as commanded by God, by the hand of Moses. At this point, the children of Israel have received the commandment to give of all the first fruits of the land. Of every tree producing fruit or of the vegetables they grow for food. There is a reason for such a law, to make sure that everyone has food for their bodies and basic provisions for life. The tithe is a progressive law for the children of Israel, as seen in Numbers 18:21 and Deuteronomy 26:12.

Numbers 18:21 reads: *"And, behold, I have given the children of Levi **all the tenth** in Israel for an **inheritance**, for their service which they serve, even the service of the tabernacle of the congregation."*

This verse tells us the original intent of the tithe, to provide for those serving in the ministry. A job that requires much time, to make sure the Levites have provision that they otherwise might not have ample supply of because they serve full time in God's house. Also, observe the specificity of whom this law is written to, Israel. Another point in this is; the tithe, at this juncture, is food products, not money. Another point about tithing that ministers never mention is that, tithing is an act that has a specific time of observation.

Deuteronomy 26:12 says: *"When thou hast made an end of tithing all the tithes of **thine increase the third year**, which is the **year of tithing**, and hast given it unto the Levite, the stranger, the fatherless, and the widow, that they **may eat** within thy gates, and be **filled**;"*

This verse tells us the specific reasons for the tithe; it is food stuffs given to the church to support the caretakers of the services, and all of the other persons listed in the above verse. The tithe is a means to assure that everyone has food to eat, to his or her satiety (To eat until full). Did you catch the progressiveness of how the tithe is to be used? It started out as an heritage for the Levites and has reached out to the fatherless, the widow, and the stranger. Realizing that in today's world, just bringing in farm products would not sustain our modern day needs in supporting the church, though the tithe, in its original order was not money. Today money is necessary in helping others to move forward in addition to other goods.

Food product's alone is not sufficient to help someone, who needs to keep their lights on, or have transportation to a doctor's appointment. Pay particular attention to the section of this verse that states, *"thine increase the third year,"* The tithe was collected every 3 years and brought into the storehouse. It was distributed out to the people as needed. Again, in modern times, some things would not work today, as in the days of old. Only giving to the church every 3 years is not a feasible or reasonable way to support the church or charity organizations of today.

The tithe changed from that of supporting the Levites, to that of helping many in need of assistance, including the stranger visiting Israel. The beginning of tithing was about supporting the full time staff of God's house of worship.

In Saint Matthew 23:23, we find the words of Jesus to the scribes and Pharisees concerning their hypocrisy.

*"Woe unto you, scribes and Pharisees, hypocrites! for ye pay **tithe of mint and anise and cummin**, and have **omitted** the weightier matters of the **law**, judgment, mercy, and faith: these ought ye to have done, and not to leave the other undone."*

The scribes and Pharisees are operating under the law, which includes the paying of tithes. Our Lord and Savoir Jesus Christ is rebuking that methodology. The scribes and Pharisees pay tithes but are not fair and just in their decisions; they have no love in their hearts for others; and more importantly, they have no faith in Christ. Jesus is telling them that under the law, they have only done a small portion of the law by paying tithes. The other matters of the law are more important. The fact is, you can give all of your possessions to charity, the church, and etcetera; however, without love, faith, and compassion, paying tithes comes to naught. The word *"Woe"* means grief. In other words, Jesus is letting them know that, unless they come into subjection of the true Gospel, and do right by the people, destruction is your reward; your tithes are null and void. There is a mystery of Christ hidden in Matthew 23:23, and that mystery is this; Jesus said to the scribes and Pharisees, yes, you should pay the tithe as required by the law. Yet, in Hebrews 7:18, it says the law is disannulled, which includes the tithe. Don't be confused, the revelation of the mystery is this; Christ had not fulfilled His mission on earth. Until Jesus died upon that tree and then being resurrected from the dead, we were still under the law. Now, in the resurrected Christ, the law is out and we are under grace. Glory to God!

After Jesus' death, and resurrection we are under grace, no more law. This can be substantiated even further by the Scriptures. The tribe of Levi was not counted in the twelve tribes of Israel because they had been set aside by God as the caretakers of the church. However, the tribe of Dan did an awful thing and was eliminated as a tribe by God. After Jesus' resurrection the tribe of Levi is now counted as one of the twelve tribes again. Examine the following books to see the entire picture: Numbers, Chapter 12; 1 Kings 12:28-31, 1 Kings 15:20; 2 Kings 10:29, and Revelation, Chapter 7.

Now let us examine Malachi 3:10:

*"Bring ye all the tithes into the storehouse, that there may be **meat in mine house**, and prove me now herewith, saith the LORD of hosts, if I will not open you the windows of heaven, and pour you out a blessing, that there shall not be room enough to receive it."*

For our study in this lesson, the main point of this verse is, *"meat in mine house,"* This reiterates the fact that the original tithe is food products, not money. The meaning of the word *"meat"* in this verse comes from the prime root word "taraph": to supply with food. Do not get tithing confused; do not give just to receive. We must give earnestly from the goodness of our hearts, otherwise, giving becomes of none effect. Turn to Saint Luke 18:10-14, the parable of the self-righteous person:

*"Two men went up into the temple to pray; the one a Pharisee, and the other a publican. 11 The Pharisee stood and prayed thus **with himself**, God, I thank thee, that I am not as other men are, extortioners, unjust, adulterers, or even as this publican. 12 I fast twice in the week, **I give tithes of all that I possess**. 13 And the publican, standing afar off, would not lift up so much as his eyes unto heaven, but smote upon his breast, saying, **God be merciful to me a sinner**. 14 I tell you, this man went down to his house justified rather than the other: for every one that exalteth himself shall be abased; and he that humbleth himself shall be exalted."*

The Pharisee in this verse is a self-righteous hypocrite, believing he is above other people. He is boasting about what he does and does not do, and not really understanding the process of Christianity. The publican humbled himself and paid respect unto God. Jesus is letting us know that, though the Pharisee has some moral values, he lacks humility and understanding of the ways of godly living.

The point being, the Pharisee, though he pays tithes is lost for lack of understanding. The publican, though he might not have much or consider himself of esteem, recognizes that, God must be honored above all else and confesses his sins. Folks, we cannot pay our way into heaven.

The tithe is based upon a law received of Moses under the old priesthood teachings, and commandments, to keep the people in line with what God required them to do in order to be saved. It did not work because the blood of goats and bulls, and so forth, all had fault in them. We needed a priesthood that is perfect and undefiled. Turn to Hebrews, Chapter 7. We will discuss verses 12-22.

Hebrews 7:12:22: *"For the **priesthood being changed**, there is made of **necessity** a **change also of the law**. 13 For he of whom these things are spoken pertaineth to another tribe, of which **no man** gave attendance at the altar. 14 For it is evident that our **Lord sprang out of Juda**; of which tribe **Moses spake nothing concerning priesthood**. 15 And it is yet far more evident; for that after the similitude of Melchisedec there **ariseth another priest**, 16 Who is made, **not after the law** of a **carnal commandment**, but after the power of an **endless life**. 17 For he testifieth, Thou art a priest for ever after the order of Melchisedec. 18 For there is verily a **disannulling** of the commandment going before for the **weakness and unprofitableness** thereof. 19 For the **law made nothing perfect**, but the bringing in of a **better hope did**; by the which we **draw nigh unto God**. 20 And inasmuch as not without an oath he was made priest: 21 (For those priests were made without an oath; but this with an oath by him that said unto him, The Lord sware and will not repent, **Thou art a priest for ever after the order of***

Melchisedec:*) 22 By so much* was **_Jesus made a surety_** *of a better testament."*

In the old priesthood, under the law, the sacrifice of animals was required to be in compliance with the rules of God, for forgiveness of sin. It did not work and the process had to be repeated over and over again because we are all sinners and come short of the glory of God. Moreover, God loves the animals HE created also, and the animals were being slaughtered regularly for man, who always sins. Thousands, if not millions of animals were slaughtered for the purpose of cleansing the people. God loves all of HIS creations and decided to make a change in the law, of *"necessity"* because HE changed the priesthood in order to have a Permanent Sacrifice for salvation.

Changing the priesthood and the law, changed many other conditions as well: no more innocent animals slaughtered for sacrifices; no more men, who have infirmity in them, making intercession for other men; and most importantly, the establishment of the True Vine, as the Intercessor for the forgiveness of our sins.

The tribe of Judah, the bloodline of Jesus Christ, was not included in the law of tithes. The law of tithing pertained to the Levitical priesthood, that is why Moses did not speak to the tribe of Judah about the priesthood. Melchisedec was a man of perfection in the eyes of God, but Melchisedec operated under the law that was to be changed and a New Priesthood established. Because Melchisedec was under the law, the New Priest, not under the law of a *"carnal commandment,"* brought in a *"better testament"* for all of the people, a priesthood, filled with life eternal that both the life and the New Priesthood will never end.

The old law, under Moses, as presented by Moses did not work in bringing souls to God. The Holy Bible is perfectly clear in over turning the old law. The words **disannulling, unprofitableness, and weakness**, leave no doubt, that the old law is out, and a New Priesthood has been established. The old law failed in that souls were not brought to God: *"law made nothing perfect; better hope did; draw nigh unto God."* Jesus, the Son of God, became the New Priest, with an assuredness, that all, who believe on Him, would have life eternally.

We serve a great loving and just God. The people living prior to Jesus coming to earth and teaching, being crucified, and then ascending up to heaven had to have the same opportunity to hear the true gospel, as those of us living after the coming of our Lord and Savior Jesus Christ. Turn to 1Peter 3:18-19:

*"For Christ also hath once suffered for sins, the just for the unjust, that he **might bring us to God**, being put to death in the flesh, **but quickened by the Spirit**: 19 By which also he went **and preached unto the spirits in prison**;"*

Our Father in heaven sent HIS only Begotten Son, to be a sacrifice for every human being that will ever live the life of flesh and blood upon the earth. Therefore, when Jesus was crucified and put into that tomb, the Holy Spirit went and *"quickened"* Him, that is, brought Him to life in the spirit, so He could complete His mission.

The old law did not work; however, the New Priest is surety for all souls to have the same opportunity for eternal life, *"might bring us to God,"* for all, who believe on Jesus Christ. For all those, who lived, before His coming and all that live after His coming. The paying of tithes will not get anyone into heaven. We must try to live a Christian life, believing on the name of the Lord Jesus Christ.

In 2 Corinthians 9:6-7, we find another very significant fact about our giving:

*"But this I say, He which soweth sparingly shall reap also sparingly; and he which soweth bountifully shall reap also bountifully. 7 Every man according as he **purposeth in his heart**, so let him give; **not grudgingly**, or of **necessity**: for God loveth a cheerful giver."*

The Holy Bible does not contradict itself in any way, form, or fashion, from the first cover of the Old Testament, to the last cover of the New Testament. The old law was taken away in the blood of Jesus. The New Covenant established in the blood of Jesus, does not require a specific amount of money or property to be given to the church. Our salvation has nothing to do with tithing, but rather, our belief on Jesus Christ. What we give to others must be given as a free gift from the heart. The old law of tithing was changed of *"necessity"* in order to bring souls to God. Many, who paid tithes under the law, did it for show or with malice in their hearts about what they gave.

In Malachi 3:1-3, the LORD GOD is sending a message to the people that HE is going to make a change in how salvation is to be achieved, not by the old law, but rather, under a New Covenant, under the Messenger of the covenant. Those, who are willing and able to understand will comply with the new rules and be made whole, they will be refined and shine like silver and gold tried in the fire.

Now turn to 2 Corinthians, Chapter 9. There you will find Paul's words about giving, which says nothing about tithing. The entire chapter is about giving. There was an abundance of supplies given to help everyone. In verse 9:13 it states:

*"Whiles by the experiment of this ministration they glorify God for your professed subjection unto the **gospel of Christ**, and for your **liberal distribution** unto them, and unto all men;"*

It is like this, my Christian friends, the first thing we all have to do is, to be believers of the Gospel of Jesus Christ. If we have Jesus in us, our giving will be from the love in our hearts for Him and for our fellow man. What we give has to be from the heart, freely given, not of necessity for salvation. The *"liberal distribution"* of what we have will supply the needs of all people. Just think what a wonderful world it would be if every human being on earth had food, clothing, and shelter, because we all shared in what we have.

Galatians 3:10: *"For as many as are of the **works of the law** are under the **curse**: for it is written, **Cursed is every one** that **continueth not in all things** which are written in the **book of the law to do them**."*

This verse is monumental in content to all Christians, who continue to tithe following the law. This verse outright states that, if you follow the law, but not the entire law, you are *"Cursed."* If you are following the rule of tithing, you are following part of the law. You must continue to sacrifice animals and to do all of things of the old law to achieve salvation, which you will fail. Let them, who have ears to hear and eyes to see, have their understanding opened up. The Bible does not lie! Don't curse your life by acting under part of the old law. Profess Jesus as Lord and Savior, and give freely from your heart.

The how we are to give is simple, freely from the heart, *"a cheerful giver."* What are we to give? Clothing, food, money, shelter, and whatever we have that can benefit someone in need. To whom do we give? The church, charities, our neighbors, our friends and or enemies, strangers and family members, and anyone needing assistance. Don't get this confused. Those who don't try to help themselves, are not to be given a free ride through life. Able bodied people are to work in someway or another. Those, who don't work, don't eat.

Having the Book of Malachi; as the last word in the Old Testament, before the New Testament, did not happen by chance. The Book of Malachi is the closeout of the old ways, leading into the New Covenant. It tells us some of the history of the old ways and introduces us to the New Covenant, under Jesus Christ.

Whatever you give, give it to the honor and glory of God, in the name of our Lord and Savior, Jesus Christ, for the up-building of HIS Kingdom. Glory to God, hallelujah to HIS name. Amen.

Review Questions:

1. The question in Malachi 3:8 says that we rob God in:

a. Tithes
b. Offerings
c. Tithes and Offerings
d. Service

2. Melchizedek received tithes of Abram:

a. True
b. False

3. Abram was very rich in silver and gold:

a. True
b. False

4. Ten percent of all the first fruits, whether of the tree or the land is the LORD'S:

a. True
b. False

5. All of the tithe was initially given to the Levites for what reason:

a. An inheritance
b. Their service of the tabernacle

c. The children of Israel
d. Both a and b

6. Deuteronomy 26:12 says the year of tithing is:

a. The first year
b. Every payday
c. The third year

7. In the third year of tithing, the tithe is intended to feed the Levite, the stranger, the fatherless, and the widow:

a. True
b. False

8. In Matthew 23:23, Jesus tells the scribes and Pharisees that tithing of mint, anise, and cummin, or greater matters than judgment, mercy, and faith:

a. True
b. False

9. In St. Luke 18:10-14, it is better to fast and tithe rather than confessing to be a sinner:

a. True
b. False

10. In Hebrews 7:12-22, the old priesthood is changed and to be clearly understood, the Scripture used all of the followings words except:

a. Blessed
b. Disannulling
c. Unprofitableness
d. Weakness

11. Under the New Covenant, we are to give from our heart, cheerfully, not of necessity, or grudgingly:

a. True
b. False

12. Galatians 3:10 says, that to continue in part of the old law and not following the whole law is a:

a. Blessing
b. Christian responsibility
c. Curse

ABOUT THE AUTHOR

Anthony J. Vance is a consistent and avid student of the Holy Scriptures. He has previously served as the president of the Baptist Training Union of his church in Arkansas, and he is a retired member of the United States military. He is actively engaged in becoming a doctor of theology.

HONOR GOD

1. b   2. e   3. a   4. b   5. d   6. b   7. b   8. c

THE BEST WE CAN OFFER

1. a   2. a   3. d   4. c   5. a   6. b   7. b

PRAY TOWARD HEAVEN

1. c   2. a   3. a   4. a

TO PRAISE or TO FORSAKE

1. a   2. a   3. a   4. c   5. b   6. a

BEAUTIFUL HOUSE of WORSHIP

1. d   2. b   3. a   4. a   5. b   6. a   7. a

A MAN OF GREAT FAITH

1. a   2. a   3. b   4. b   5. c

EVIL GAIN, ONLY TO LOSE

1. b   2. a   3. a   4. b   5. a   6. b   7. b

CREATURES OF GOD'S LOVE

1. a   2. a   3. c   4. a   5. a

LIVING GODLY

1. a   2. b   3. c   4. b   5. b

THE FIRST CHILDREN

1. a   2. a   3. c   4. a   5. a

HEAVEN BOUND

1. d   2. a   3. a   4. a   5. a

PLENTIOUS BOUNTY IN SHARING

1. b   2. c   3. a   4. a   5. a

THE IMMUTABLE GOD

1. c   2. d   3. a   4. a   5. a   6. d

3

A CITY LOST, TYRUS or ATLANTIS

1. a   2. b   3. b   4. c   5. a   6. c   7. a   8. b

NOT JUST A FIERY FURNACE

1. a   2. a   3. b   4. d   5. a   6. d   7. a

THE FEROCIOUS MOUTH TAMED

1. c   2. d   3. c   4. a   5. b   6. b   7. d.   8. a
9. a   10. c

PREACHING TO THE LOST

1. c   2. c   3. a   4. c   5. a

WHAT DO I GIVE

1. c   2. a   3. a   4. a   5. d   6. c   7. a   8. b
9. b   10. a   11. a   12. c

www.ingramcontent.com/pod-product-compliance
Lightning Source LLC
Chambersburg PA
CBHW030942180526
45163CB00002B/669